Take a walk in my shoes

Based on a true story

By: D M Cummings

This book is a work of fiction. Names, characters, and places and incidents are products of the author's imagination or are used fictitiously. Any resemblance to actual events or locales or persons, living or dead, is entirely coincidental.

The World Is Mine (TWIM) Publishing
P.O. Box 3086
Akron, OH 44309

Copyright 2014 by D M Cummings

All rights reserved,
including the right of reproduction
in whole or in part in any form

ISBN: 978-0-9773854-2-3

Cover designed by A. P. Bolden

-Revised 2023-

Manufactured in the United States of America

Acknowledgements

First and always, I would like to thank God for his blessings and for giving me the strength, power and ability to be able to sit down and write a book. To my parents thank you for everything, especially for raising me to be an independent and respectful person. I would like to thank my oldest daughter for keeping an eye on my little ladies while I ventured off into this story. To my baby girl, for her doing a wonderful job on the book cover with her beautiful legs, to my middle daughter thanks for being the sweet and loving person you are. And to the lady whom this story is based on, thank you for giving me the opportunity to tell your story, you've been through a lot, and it takes a strong person to talk about it.

Prologue

1958 in Russellville, Alabama, John Woods, a light skinned young man, with pretty, Indian hair that he inherited from his Indian mother, was relaxing in his one-bedroom apartment on his orange and brown couch that was handed down from his parents, watching a western on his 26" black and white television, when he heard a knock on his door.
"John Woods this is the county sheriff please open the door." John, who was very slim, weighing about 165 pounds and stood about 5'8, jumped up knocking the package of Zig Zags that was lying on the couch onto the floor and brushed the wrinkles out of his clothes, thinking *what the sheriff could be doing at his house.* His beautiful wife Vivian, and their three children, Gale, James and Cassandra were at the market, and he prayed nothing had happened to his family. John cracked the door open enough just to peek his head out; there was no screen on the door so when he looked out, they were face to face.

"Yes sir, how may I help you? John asked distraught.
"I need you to step outside for just a moment, or may I come?" John stepped outside with no shoes and socks which was fine for this eighty-degree weather.
"What's the problem officer? Is it my wife and kids?" The officer flipped through a stack papers.
"Hmm, are you any relation to a…Pearl Jameson?"
"Yes, that's my sister, why?" James asked with fear in his eyes.
"There's-- been an accident. We need you at the County hospital ASAP." John stood there dumbfounded.
"Is…Is everything alright?" he asked slowly.
"I'm not sure sir, just get to the hospital as soon as you can."

Chapter 1

"Dad, what's the matter?" Cassandra asked her whimpering father who was sitting with his left hand covering his forehead showing bruised knuckles and scared up hands from doing manly duties and whatever else he did. She always thought that once a man turned a certain age he stopped crying, until one afternoon she came home from school and her father was sitting at the kitchen table with a bottle of Bourbon, no cup, but drinking straight from the bottle. His eyes were blood shot and tears were streaming down his face. She sat at the table hoping to get an answer.

"Cassandra, just go to your room," she didn't ask any more questions. She got up with tears in her eyes, hurting because her father was hurting. She later learned that her Uncle Linny, his brother, had been killed gambling at a card game. Her father, John, had walked into the house and saw his limp body lying across the table and he felt it was his fault because he was supposed to have been there earlier but had stopped at the store for a twelve pack of Budweiser and a pack of Zig Zags. The last few years had really been stressful for John, and this was just the last straw. His sister had been shot in the head a few years earlier in Russellville, Alabama, by her husband, which was the reason John now lived in Ohio. He arrived at County Hospital to be escorted to a room to identify his sister's body. John cried for days. He had asked his sister to leave her husband on several occasions, but down south love is deeper than anyone would ever know. One year after his sister's death John packed up his wife and kids and moved to Ohio to rid his mind of the place that took his sister. The following year John watched his father, Paul, who had a serious drinking problem, suffer and then finally die from blood clots and cirrhosis of the liver. John had begun to drink a lot too, that was the only way he was happy, although everyone around him was miserable.

When John was sober, he was loved by everyone in the neighborhood. Cassandra, who was a splitting image of her Aunt Pearl, always felt fortunate because she had both of her parents and they were still together. They had a beautiful white house with green shutters. There were two bedrooms' downstairs, the master bedroom with the bathroom was for her mother and father, and the other was a guest room. There was a finished attic that Cassandra and her siblings shared that contained two bedrooms, one for Cassandra and her younger sister Gale, and the other was for her younger brother James. There was an extended hallway where a couch sat for their relaxation. Their attic also had a bathroom with a shower, and they swore it was haunted. They always thought that they heard ghosts. There would be times when they would be in their rooms and they would hear someone walking up the stairs with a chain and a bucket, but they never saw anyone. They would run outside screaming and their father was right there with his shot gun. They had a one car garage where they parked their blue 1967 Nova with blue, tan and black checkered seats. John worked at a machine shop twenty minutes away from their home and her mother worked as a cashier at a convenient store three blocks away, so she walked to work, and he drove the Nova.

They had a huge garden in their backyard that consisted of Collard and Turnip greens, potatoes, tomatoes, all kinds of peppers, squash, peas, cabbage, green beans, pumpkins and watermelons, and every Saturday morning John and James would get up around four thirty in the morning and go fishing and hunting for deer, rabbit, raccoon and possum. There were chickens running around the yard that they watched grow up and later had to eat, so they never looked at them as pets. They ate well every day and so did the single mothers in the neighborhood. John was so free-spirit and had a big heart. He would take some of the boys in the neighborhood on hayrides around Halloween, let them go fishing with them some evenings when he was going for fun, and he allowed them to pick vegetables out of his garden to make sure their family had a good meal too.

    Gale always thought she was so much prettier than Cassandra because she was lighter complected. They both had long pretty hair that their mother, Vivian kept neatly pressed. Gale always wore her hair down with pretty Shirley Temple curls and Cassandra either wore her hair in a ponytail or just combed to the back. Gale had a little shape and wore pretty dresses and short skirts, and Cassandra usually wore jeans and a big sweater, but when she got dressed and did her hair, she was beautiful, and Gale would become upset when people would complement her. Every evening when Cassandra got out of school, she would go home, water the garden and pick anything that had harvested. She would take the food into the house and clean it. She'd soak the greens so her mother could cut them up, freeze them, snap any peas and green beans and freeze them while Gale sat in her room polishing her nails and doing her hair while listening to the radio. Cassandra always asked Gale for help, but she never helped her.

    One afternoon Cassandra came into the house after picking vegetables from the garden, pouring in sweat and ready for a hot shower. She went towards the bathroom and the door was locked. She knocked.

"Yes?" asked an unfamiliar voice. Cassandra looked into their bedroom and Gale was lying on her bed polishing her nails.
"Who is that?" Cassandra asked. Gale shrugged her shoulders.
"It's Auntie Joyce."
"What is she doing over here?"
"I don't know, but she's been in there for a while." Gale said as she sat up on the bed to dry her pink nail polish. "And her kids Tanya and Travon are here too." Cassandra hadn't noticed them when she came home from school. She sat in the chair in her bedroom with her dirty blue jean shorts and a spotted blue t-shirt and waited for her aunt to come out of the bathroom because no one was allowed to shower in her parents' shower. She waited a half an hour and Joyce finally came out of the bathroom and went downstairs and into the living room. Cassandra got up to get her robe and a change of under clothes and when she walked towards the bathroom the door was closed again and again, she knocked on the door.
"Yeah?" asked her cousin Tanya.
"Are you going to be long?" Cassandra asked after a long sigh.
"I just need to take a shower and then I'll be out."
"Oh my Gosh!" yelled Cassandra as she walked back to her bedroom. She took off all her clothes except for her panties and bra and

put on her robe. She lied across her bed and listened to the radio with Gale.

"Why are they all over here taking showers?" asked Cassandra.

"I don't know, but they had a lot of bags too. I think they are moving in, and Tanya is going to be sleeping in your bed and Travon in there with James."

"Oh, hell no! This house is too small for all of them to fit. They gon' eat up all our food, especially Travon's greedy ass. Why can't they go to their own house?" Cassandra shrugged her shoulders. Tanya came out of the bathroom and laid across Cassandra's bed. Cassandra rolled her eyes and ran into the bathroom before anyone else made their way in there. Cassandra turned on the water and, of course, it was cold. They had used up all the hot water. She quickly rinsed her body in cool water; she lathered some soap on her rag and quickly washed her body. She rinsed off again and got out – a quick three-minute shower. An hour later, Vivian, who was also light skinned with high cheek bones and beautiful long hair that she wore in curls, came home from work and freshened up. She always made sure that she had on her makeup and that she was flawless. Auntie Joyce had put some coon in the oven, cut up some potatoes, and was about to fry some corn, so for the first time in years, Vivian was able to come home and sit down to relax.

Auntie Joyce finished the food, and they sat down and ate without John who was almost an hour late coming home. The girls cleaned up the kitchen while Vivian dozed off on the couch watching M*A*S*H. John came home from work drunk, as always. He knew that Auntie Joyce and her kids were going to stay with them for a while and he wasn't thrilled about it, but Vivian was known for letting people stay in their home when they were down on their luck. She wouldn't allow anyone to be homeless as long as she had a roof over her head. When John walked through the kitchen, he saw the food in containers on the stove and the dishes all washed and put away, so he knew that everyone had eaten without him.
"Where is Vivian?" asked John without speaking to their guest.
"I'm fine and you? Anyway, she's in there on the couch getting some well-deserved rest", said Auntie Joyce rolling her eyes. She couldn't stand John and wished that Vivian would leave him. John walked into the living room and pulled Vivian off of the couch by her feet and she hit her head on the edge of the couch before hitting the floor.
"What the hell?" Vivian yelled as she opened her eyes.
"Oh, since you got your little bitch ass sister over here, you couldn't wait for me before ya'll ate dinner?"
"What are you talking about? You are late. We ate dinner over an hour ago." John

smacked her on the side of her face. "I know you not talking back." He kicked Vivian in her side, and she grabbed his foot. "Bitch, get up and fix my plate." Vivian just sat there, and John snatched her up by her hair and when she began to scream and punch him anywhere her fist landed, he smacked her again and had just balled up his fist to punch her in the face when James and Trevon ran to her rescue. Trevon, who was light brown and stood about 6'2" weighting about 200 pounds, grabbed John by his shoulder and pulled him away from Vivian, whose mouth was bleeding. John turned around and swung at Trevon, who ducked. "Everybody is always on her side", yelled John. Trevon tackled him to the ground as Auntie Joyce, Cassandra, Gale and Cousin Tanya ran into the living room.

"Mom are you alright?" asked Gale as she kissed her mother. "Mom, I'm so tired of this, let's get out of here." Auntie Joyce knew that John beat Vivian, but she didn't know it was this bad. She had to help her sister but didn't know how without killing her husband. Two days later Aunt Joyce came home and found Vivian passed out on the kitchen floor. There was blood everywhere.

"Vivian!" Joyce yelled as she ran over to her sister. She lifted her head and blood poured out of her mouth. "Oh my gosh! Vivian are you alright?" Vivian opened her eyes and when she saw her sister a smile came across her face; she knew she was safe.

"Come on Vivian we are going to the hospital."
"No, I'm fine", said Vivian as she struggled to get up off the floor.
"Why do you continue to let this drunk bastard beat on you like this?" asked Joyce.
"I love him, and the kids need him. We can't survive if he leaves us, and the preacher said until death do us part."
"Yeah, and that goes both ways, and I hope it's not till *your* death do *you* part."

    Joyce put Vivian in the car and took her to University Hospital, where they kept her overnight. John came to the hospital acting so concerned, more concerned about her pressing charges. Vivian told them she had fallen down the basement steps. She loved John and needed him to help support their three kids. When Vivian came home, she went straight to bed to get some rest because the doctors had bothered her all night and didn't allow her to sleep. She took a couple of days off work to let her bruises heal. Vivian ran her a hot bath with Epsom salts so that she could soak her aching body.

    Auntie Joyce called their mother Rose Ann, who lived in Alabama.
"Hey, mama this is Joyce."
"Oh, hey baby. I haven't heard from you in a while. Is everything alright?"
"No mama. John has been beating the crap out of Vivian. She just came home from the

hospital. I've been staying here because I was having a hard time at my place and we got evicted, but that's a whole 'nother story. I came home and she was lying on the floor bleeding. It scared me to death. I took her to the hospital, and they just released her today. She's sitting around here looking a mess, and she still won't leave him."
"Where is she?"
"I think she's in the bathroom soaking her body."
"Let me speak to her."
"Mama, she'll be mad that I called you. I want to help her, but I just don't know how." Joyce began to cry.
"I don't give a damn if she knows that you called me, she don't let that ole' drunk beat on her like that. Where are the kids?"
"They're at school right now, but they were here the other day and he almost hit my baby, who was trying to pull him off of Vivian."
"You know what? I don't want to speak to her because obviously talking is not going to work with her. Your father and I will be there next week. Are you and the kids still staying there?"
"Yes ma'am."
"Well, you protect her the best way that you can without getting yourself hurt. I'm going to let your uncle Rodney stay in the house and we'll stay for a couple of weeks, so make some room so we can be comfortable."

"Alright mama, I'll see you soon. I love you." They hung up and Joyce went to check on Vivian.

That Saturday Grandma Rose and Grandpa Clifton came to Vivian's rescue. Aunt Joyce, as directed, had fixed the attic up nice so they could be comfortable and to give them some privacy. She took the basement where she also kept her and her kids belongings, and the kids all had to sleep either in the kitchen or the living room floor because no one was allowed to lay on the tan couch with brown legs that was covered in plastic that stuck to your body when you sat on it. Grandma Rose brought enough luggage for several months, you would have thought they were moving in. Vivian was surprised to see her parents because she had only seen them twice since she moved from Alabama eight years ago. She was especially excited to see her mother who looked good at sixty-two. Vivian knew that she was safe now.

Chapter 2

One afternoon Cassandra walked home from school with some of the kids from the neighborhood as she did every day. Gale was cheerleading and John and Trevon both played football, so they stayed after. Cassandra went upstairs to her bedroom to change her clothes so that she could go outside to work in the garden as she did every day. She put on a pair of cutoff jeans and a big t-shirt. She came downstairs and was on her way out the door when her father called her name.
"Cassandra."
"Yes dad?" she answered as she rolled her eyes; she was not in the mood for any of his mess. It was about 3:45 in the afternoon and he usually left for work around 4:30 pm.
 "Come here right now!" Cassandra walked slowly to her parent's bedroom, thinking what she could have done to have her father raising his voice at her. She pulled open the ajar door and stuck her head in.
 "Yes?"
 "Come on in." She did as she was instructed. "So, what is this I hear about you losing your virginity to one of these losers in the neighborhood?"
 "Dad, I don't even have a boyfriend, and I don't go anywhere but outside in the garden."
"Um hum, lie down and take off your shorts."

"Dad, I'm not doing that anymore. I'm too old for you to be looking at my private parts. I'd rather wait 'til mom gets home." She said as she crossed her arms across her chest. Her father would periodically make her take off her underpants and would look at her vagina saying he was just making sure nobody was bothering her when in reality, he was the real pervert. Now that Cassandra was fourteen and developing, she was tired of it.
"So, are you tryna disobey me?" He asked as he grabbed her shirt and laid her on the bed.
"No, I'm not dad I just don't think this is right." Tears began to roll down her cheeks.
"Take off your shorts and let me see if you've been tampered with." Cassandra hesitantly did as she was told as she began to cry harder.
"And you can stop all those crocodile tears, because if you're lying, I'm going to beat the hell out of you."
John looked at her vagina and became instantly turned on. Cassandra was still a virgin. He stuck his finger inside of her, and she pushed away.
"I'm telling mom!" She yelled as she tried to get off the bed.
"You better not tell anyone, especially your grandfather, if you want the family to stay together. If I leave here ya'll be poor as hell and your grandfather will disown you for being so disgraceful and shaming the family." John went to his closet and pulled out an old suit, it looked like it hadn't been worn in at least ten

years. He went into the jacket pocket where a blue handkerchief hung from the pocket and took out a condom. When Cassandra saw that she got up and quickly ran for the door but was caught by the back of her shirt and he laid her back on the bed and held her with one hand while he used his other to put the condom on his erect penis. He tried to penetrate her but her small body wouldn't allow him. He tried for several minutes as Cassandra cried.

"Dad, you're hurting me. Why are you doing this to me? I thought you loved me."

"I do love you, and I'm going to show you how you are supposed to be treated and loved. You are my favorite and that's why you're getting this."

"Well, I wish you would hate me!" He ignored her comment and went to the dresser and got some Vaseline, he rubbed it on her tight vagina and squeezed his grown man hood into her immature body. Cassandra began to cry as she tried to push his heavy body off top of her, but it was no use, she could smell the alcohol with every breath that he took. She hated her father even more today than she did when he beat her mother. John's pace began to speed up as he moaned loudly. He lay atop of her for a few seconds then remembering that it was a child, his child, that he was lying on, and when he heard her whimpering, he jumped up.

"Shut up all that crying, you are now a woman. Go in the bathroom and clean yourself up. And remember, if you don't want to be homeless or have your grandfather and everybody else disowning you, this must remain our secret." Cassandra laid there for a minute staring into space. Her little body was sore, and she didn't want to move. "I said get yo lil' ass up and get cleaned up!" Cassandra jumped up and ran upstairs to her grandparent's bathroom and cried some more as she got a change of clothes. There was blood running down her leg and she knew that what her father had done to her was wrong, but how could she tell and not mess up the family? She went into the bathroom and locked the door. She got into the shower and tried to scrub away the thought of her father inside of her. She stayed in there until the water turned cold hoping that when she came out, he would be gone for work. Cassandra went into her grandparent's bedroom where she cried herself to sleep and was awakened several hours later by her sister.

"Damn Cassandra, get your lazy ass up, you ain't even work in the garden today. What's wrong with you, you pregnant? I'm telling mom and dad is going to kick your ass." Cassandra looked at her sister and began to cry all over again.

"What's wrong with you?" She smacked her lips. "You are so whack." Gale went downstairs leaving her sister upstairs to cry alone. "Mom, something is wrong with Cassandra, she up there crying. She probably pregnant," and she began to laugh.

Vivian went upstairs to check on her daughter, and when Cassandra saw her mother's black eye and swollen lip, she knew this was not the time to worry her with her problems, it was obvious she had enough of her own.
"What's wrong, baby? Why are you crying?"
"It's nothing mama, just had a bad day."
"You want to talk about it?"
"No, it's nothing you can do about it now. I'll figure it out on my own." Cassandra hugged her mother and wiped her tears. Usually, Vivian wouldn't let things go that easily, but Cassandra was right, she had too many problems of her own.

    The next day Cassandra tried her best to block out what her father had done to her, but she found herself drifting off a lot in school. When she went home that afternoon, her father raped her again. This went on for the next couple of days. Finally, Cassandra stopped coming home. She would stay after and watch Gale cheer or her brother and cousin play football. She would read a book, do her homework or just stare off into space. Everyone noticed a change in Cassandra, but no one could figure out what her problem was. One day on the way home she and Gale were walking together actually acting like sisters, Cassandra watching her cheer and walking home with her everyday had kind of brought

them closer. They were walking, talking and laughing when Cassandra decided it would be best if she told someone about her father raping her because she had been holding it in for so long that it was beginning to make her sick, but that only tore their relationship back up.
"Really Cassandra, do you really have to make up lies just to get attention? Do you know what this can do to our family?"
"Gale, I would…."
"I don't want to hear anymore." Gale interrupted and walked away, and they didn't speak the remainder of the week.

Chapter 3

Cassandra was now a senior in high school and decided that she needed something to do so that she could ease her mind from the flashbacks that she continued to have of her father raping her and showing no fatherly love for her, so she decided to join the track team. Cassandra was really good and when she ran, she felt free, everything inside of her just came out into her running. She placed every track meet, it may not have been first, but she was always in the top three. All the attention that she received from her teammates made her feel needed and loved.

One afternoon Cassandra came home from school earlier than usual because she had the worst stomachache; it was more like a cramp in the middle of her stomach. Her father was in the living room reading the newspaper and listening to the television, and her mother was in the kitchen preparing supper. She walked through the side door and into the kitchen.
"Why aren't you at school?" Her mother asked in a whisper hoping her husband didn't hear her.
"I don't know; I'm having severe abdomen pain."
"Where does it hurt? Is it cramps?"

"No, it's right above my navel and every time I move it gets worse."
"Do you need to go to the hospital?" By this time Cassandra was crying.
"I probably should."
"John, I'm about to take Cassandra to the hospital."
"What's wrong with her?"
"Her stomach is bothering her."
"We don't have no money for no doctor bills. Give her some damn pepto bismol and make her go lay down." Cassandra went upstairs and lied down in her grandmother's bed and waited for her to come home. This was no ordinary belly ache. The pain was moving towards her lower right side of her abdomen, and every time she moved it hurt more and more. Vivian gave her a couple of aspirins also, but the pain continued. When she drank the water to rinse down the aspirin it made her feel like she had to throw up. After an hour had passed, she was not better. Vivian brought her a bowl of soup, but she had no appetite, felt nauseated, and was developing a fever. A few hours later Grandma Rose came home.
"Mama, there's something wrong with Cassandra, she has a fever and she's been up there crying for the last few hours."
"What's wrong with her?"
"She's complaining about her stomach, she won't eat, and she said it feels like she has to poop, but she can't go, and it hurts if she moves."

"Well why you didn't take her to the hospital? It sounds to me like she needs to go."
"John told me to give her pepto bismol and have her lay down." Grandma Rose looked at her over the top of her glasses, brushed passed her and went upstairs to check on her grand baby. Cassandra was still lying on her side in her grandmother's bed crying. She touched her face, and she was burning up.
"What's wrong baby?"
"My stomach hurts right above my navel and right here." She touched her lower right side.
"That's your appendix; you need to get to the hospital."
"Vivian, get up here and help this baby to the car." Vivian went upstairs and saw Cassandra and felt bad that she hadn't taken her earlier, but she didn't feel like fighting with John. She helped her down the stairs and when they reached the bottom John was standing there with his arms crossed over his chest.
"Where the hell are ya'll going?"
"To the hospital."
"I told you we ain't got no money for that shit."
"Look at her, she's sick."
"She's probably pregnant and havin' a miscarriage, let the shit pass." Grandma Rose came down the stairs.
"Boy if you don't move your ignorant ass out the way, I'll move you."
"Yo old ass ain't gon' do…" Grandpa Clifton cocked his rifle without saying a word and John just walked to his bedroom and slammed the

door. When Cassandra finally reached the hospital, her appendix had ruptured. They did immediate surgery, and she stayed in the hospital for two nights and was released. Cassandra now hated her father more than she ever had, he almost caused her to lose her life and when she came home, he showed no remorse, he just looked at her, and in return she rolled her eyes and left his presence.

Chapter 4

Track ended, and Cassandra needed something else to occupy her time. Everyone always told her how pretty she was and with her petite figure she was told that she should model. Cassandra begged her parents almost every day. She asked her father on a day that he wasn't under the influence, although it killed her inside to ask him to do anything for her and to her surprise he said 'yes'. Gale was so jealous because there were several things that she had asked to do but was always told that they couldn't afford it, for instance, she wanted to go to a vocational school to study business after graduating from high school and was filling out paper work and her parents made her get a job and pay her own way and now they were paying all of this money for Cassandra to model. Gale didn't speak to her for over a week, but Cassandra didn't care because she was so happy. During the first week of Cassandra's classes at Barbizon she met her first boyfriend, Dale. Dale was twenty-four years old, he was light brown skin, stood about 6'2" and had an athletic built and although Cassandra was a senior in high school, he found her to be very mature for her age, and he took great interest in her. Cassandra was a beautiful model – she had the walk, the talk and the smile – and they hit it off really quick.

Dale would pick Cassandra up from school every day, and, of course, Gale was jealous of that and couldn't wait to tell their parents.
"So, mom, you know that some man picks Cassandra up from school every day and taking her somewhere, and she don't be coming right home so...I wonder where they be going?"
"I know, Gale, she told me all about him, so he helps us out by taking her to modeling classes and helps her with her schoolwork if she needs it. From what I hear, he's a pretty good guy."
"Well, he looks kinda old to me. How old is he anyways?"
"Girl, mind your business. If you wouldn't act like you did towards your sister, she might tell you something about herself."
"Whatever mom!" and Gale stormed off to her room. Vivian just shook her head,
 wondering why her girls couldn't get along.

    Dale and Cassandra had been seeing each other for several months, and they both seemed to really be into each other, but there was something about him that Cassandra couldn't pinpoint. She thought he may have had a girlfriend, but she couldn't prove it. Every time she asked him, he would find a way to avoid the question, so she tried to wait it out knowing that whatever is done in the dark always comes to light. She enjoyed spending time with him and picking her up and taking her to modeling school, sure did beat catching the bus, and the only thing they had ever done was kiss, which he had to teach her. She thought the fact of him putting his tongue in her mouth was disgusting, but she did it because she thought that was what she was supposed to do, and she didn't want to appear young, immature or inexperienced.

    One Saturday afternoon, Cassandra and Dale were at his apartment. He was preparing lunch for them both and they were about to watch Star Wars. They ate, and she was leaning on his chest watching his 13-inch black and white TV. Dale kissed her on the forehead and then down to her lips and of course she kissed him back. He began to rub her breast and then began to unbutton her shirt. Cassandra pushed away and turned her head. She loved Dale, but she wasn't ready for this yet.
"What's the matter, girl?"
"I'm not ready for this."
"Girl, you know I love you. I've been picking you up from school everyday and taking you to that stupid modeling bull shit. Stop acting like a baby."
"Why are you talking to me like that, baby, I love you too, it's just that… it's just…I've been through so much. I don't know who I can trust, and my modeling is not stupid, that's something that I've been wanting to do since I was a little girl."

"What you mean? I mean... What's wrong? And what I meant by your modeling being stupid, is that you can do so much better with yourself. Talk to me, tell me what's on your mind."
"It's nothing that I really feel like talking about." And tears began to fill her eyes. Dale kissed her again as he starred into her tear-filled eyes trying to act sympathetic.
"Baby, I'm not like those young guys at your school, as a matter of fact, I'm not like any guy you'll ever meet in your life. I love you, and one day you will be my wife." That thought made Cassandra smile, so she let down her guard and made love to her man. She was so afraid that she wasn't going to like it because she hated it when her father touched her, but it was so good to her that she didn't want the moment to end. As soon as they were finished, he told her to get dressed.
"Can I take a shower or at least wash up?"
"Girl, I got stuff to do." Dale threw on some sweatpants, a wife beater t-shirt and some flip flops and sat in the living room by the door. She got up as instructed and angrily put on her clothes. They didn't talk the whole ride home. She didn't understand what had just happened. To her it was a great experience. She wanted so badly to tell someone about her experience, but she had no one to talk to and she knew that Gale would for sure tell her parents, so she got her diary that she kept tucked way

under her mattress and wrote all about it and cried herself to sleep.

    The next morning Cassandra went by Dale's, and no one answered, and the next few times was the same thing. She was hurt, but what could she do? And to add oil to the fire, one afternoon she was walking to the corner store and saw Dale and his girlfriend riding down the street. She was a girl his age that lived in the neighborhood. Cassandra gave him the middle finger, and he ignored her gesture and continued about his way. Her suspicions were right another man had broken her heart.

Chapter 5

BAM, BAM, BAM, there was a heavy knock at the door.

"James T. Woods" a military recruiter yelled from the other side of the door. James was now nineteen, soon to be twenty and was being drafted into the military. He was brown skinned, about 5'11" and very slim. John was at the bar somewhere, Grandma and Grandpa were on their daily walk, and Vivian was cooking dinner. She had no clue what to do. The recruiter who was tall, really buff with a crew cut hairstyle, waited while James did as he was instructed and gathered a few important items and he was taken away. Vivian screamed and cried.
"Please don't take my baby, take his sorry ass daddy. He is still a baby."
"Ma'am, he's going to serve his country. You should be proud of him."
"No one signed him up for this crap." Vivian hardly ever used foul language.
"Ma'am, he'll be fine. You'll hear from him in a few days."
"Mama, please don't let them take me. I'm not fit for this. I'll do whatever you need me to do, but I don't want to go to no damn army." Vivian saw tears fall from her baby's eyes. The recruiter escorted him out of the house and into a military van. Vivian cried the remainder of

the day and never finished dinner. John finally came home, and she tried to tell him, but he was too drunk to care and more concerned about his dinner not being done.

******

April 4, 1968, the day of Martin Luther King, Jr.'s assassination, a young man had just come home from the military and moved in across the street from Cassandra and her family. Cassandra had been sitting on her porch watching the moving trucks when she noticed a tall, light brown skinned brother with black curly hair and a goatee get out of the truck with his military uniform on. He appeared to be very attractive from afar, and she didn't notice a woman with him. She knew a woman stayed in that apartment, but he looked too young for her, he had to be a nephew or something. Cassandra went into the house and prepared an apple pie. Her mother always prepared a few crusts and kept them in the freezer for an emergency such as this. She got all the ingredients together and put the pie in the oven. She watched him all afternoon while her pie baked and finally decided to go over and introduce herself. She went upstairs and took an extra-long shower and put on a nice pair of short shorts, a tank top, a little make up, sprayed some of her favorite perfume, grabbed the pie and went across the street. She

knocked on the door, Eric answered, and he was even more handsome up close.
"Hello. Welcome to the neighborhood. My name is Cassandra." She said handing him the pie with a smile.
"Well good afternoon, Miss Cassandra, my name is Eric, and what do we have here? I saw you over there watching me all afternoon." Cassandra began to smile.
"Or were you watching me?" They both began to laugh, and she noticed that he had a gorgeous smile. "So, I saw all that military stuff, are you coming from the army or something?"
"Yeah, I served my time for this country, now I'm about to kick back and relax over here with my relatives before I have to go back to work."
"Ok, so are you married?"
"No not yet. I haven't met that special lady."
"Well, if you need anything feel free to come over."
"Alright, I'm going to hold you to that."
Cassandra turned and walked away putting a little twist in her hips because she knew he was watching. She walked in the house, sat on the couch, flipped on the television, and at 6:01 that evening it flashed across the screen the Martin Luther King, Jr. had been assassinated. She began to sob silently, and a few minutes later she heard a knock on the door. She didn't even wipe her tears she just dragged herself to the door and there stood Eric. She unlocked

the screen and went back to the couch. He opened the door and came in.
"I'm allowed in, right?"
"You're fine." She said between sniffles.
"Are you alright?"
"Yes, just heard about Martin Luther King, Jr. What is this world coming to?"
"Yeah, I know. I've been around so much killing and stuff these last couple of years." Eric shook his head. "Man. Well don't sit around her moping about it. I've learned that you can't change the past, and crying is not going to bring him back. I mean it helps but…" He shook his head again. "So do you want to go to the movies or something to help easy your mind?"
"That will be nice. What time does it start?"
"I don't know, do you have a newspaper?" Cassandra went into the bathroom, grabbed the newspaper off the floor, where her father usually left it after reading it every morning, and searched for the movie section. Her mind was instantly distracted. She brought the paper back to the living room and handed it to Eric. "What time is your curfew?"
"I'm out of school; I mean I graduated like two years ago, so I really don't have one."
"Alright, let's go to the drive in." Cassandra had never been to a drive in and was ecstatic. They sat and talked for a while getting to know each other before it was time to get ready to go. Eric had a nice tan, four-door Cheval equipped with an 8-track, blue and black

checkered seats, big tires and fins on the back of the car. They went to the movies, and the only thing that she could remember was the beginning of the movie. They were parked way in the back by some trees, and it was extremely dark, and it had begun to thunder and lightning, and Cassandra was afraid. They hugged, kissed and rubbed each other for at least forty-five minutes.
"Come on, let's get in the back." Eric Insisted and Cassandra didn't hesitate. They had sex for at least an hour, and she had multiple orgasms. She really wasn't sure what was going on with her body, but she knew it felt extremely good. By the middle of the second movie, they were both exhausted, so they went home. They sat in his driveway and talked for another hour before Cassandra walked across the street.
"Don't disappear," she demanded with a smirk.
"Baby, we are neighbors. Where am I going?" Cassandra went home and took a long shower feeling like a new person.
A few months had passed, and she and Eric were spending a lot of time together. She had a part time job at the local convenient store and was able to help her family with the bills. Finally, she felt she had found what was missing in her life.

******

Sunday morning everyone was sitting around having a family breakfast before they

went to church. Grandma Rose always made a big breakfast on Sundays. They had fried chicken, waffles, home fries and freshly squeezed orange juice. They all ate, and the next thing you knew Gale got up from the table and ran into the bathroom. Grandma Rose looked at Vivian and followed behind Gale, she was throwing up barely making it to the toilet.
"Um, what's wrong with you child?"
"I don't know, Grandma, something made me sick."
"You ain't been getting sick when you ate my food. What you supposed to be pregnant?"
"No ma'am, it must have been something that I ate."
"You tell them lies to somebody else. Ya best get yaself checked out. I ain't gon' tell ya mama what I know, but you better tell her so she can talk to ya crazy ass daddy so that he don't kill yo ass."
"Ok grandma, I'm gon' go get checked."
Grandma Rose made her way back into the kitchen.
"What's wrong with Gale?" John asked.
"She's fine, just a little upset stomach that's all."
"That's all that better be wrong with her." Vivian rolled her eyes at her husband's ignorant comment.

　　Gale thought that she might have been pregnant because her cycle was two weeks late, but she was hoping it was just stress.

Later that week she went to the local clinic to get a free pregnancy test and was distraught at the positive result. Gale and Brian had been dating for the past eight months and they thought that they were in love, but she refused to tell her parents because she knew that they would be disappointed in her, even though she was grown. Three months went by, and Gale's once flat stomach began to bulge and of course her father noticed immediately.
"Gale, we need to talk." *Oh gosh here we go*, she thought. "I've noticed you picking up a little weight. Is there something that you need to tell me?"
"Nope" she replied and got up and went into the room with her mother and Grandma Rose, she knew he would not go around her grandmother tripping. Grandma and Grandpa had extended their stay through the end of the summer or longer if needed.

    Gale decided she need to go ahead and tell someone, at least her mother and grandmother, that she was about to be a mother.
"So, what are you guys watching?"
"Dark Shadow. What's the matter with you?" asked Vivian.
"Oh, nothing."
"Yes, it is, Gale. What did your father want with you?"
"To get on my nerves as usual."
"Um hum."

"I'm pregnant." She blurted out. Vivian looked at Grandma Rose who rolled her eyes.
"I already knew it. I was just waiting on you to tell us, so what are you going to do?"
"I'm keeping it. What do you mean?"
"There's no question about that, I'm talking about you and that boy."
"Brian is going to help me take care of it."
"Take care of what?" John asked as he walked into the living room. The room became so quiet that you could hear a mouse piss on cotton. He looked at Gale who began to watch Dark Shadow, like she knew what was going on. "Gale...Vivian... Mama Rose...What's going on?"
"Well, Gale is pregnant." Vivian replied after a long silence.
"By that Brian guy that's been coming around here?" Gale nodded her head.
"I'm going to get my pistol and..."
"And do *what*?" Grandma Rose yelled in exasperation.
"Nobody's going to touch my daughters. I'm going to put a cap in his ass."
"Oh, how brilliant, so the baby won't have a father? How much sense does that make? You need to learn how to deal with things in a different way," said Rose.
"Alright, we need to have a family meeting with Brian."
"Why?" asked Gale.
"I need to know what his plans are."
"He said he would help take care of the baby."

"And who's going to help take care of you?"
"What do you mean?"
"Once that baby is born you gotta go. Ain't no baby that ain't mine living under my roof."
"Really?" And Gale looked at her mother and then her grandmother and neither one of them made a comment. "Helloooo... Are you really going to let him put me out?"
"Gale you are grown and obviously you want to make grown decisions, I will talk to your father, but there's probably no changing his mind. You and Brian need to go ahead and get married and raise that baby right. It's hard enough as it is, an extra mouth to feed will be a lot on this family."
"It's not like I don't have a job."
"I know baby, but you've known that's been a house rule since day one. Once you graduate from high school you can stay here as long as you want, but you have to keep a job or go to school and don't have any kids."

Gale got up and stormed out of the room in tears, she couldn't believe that her parents was actually, putting her out.

Chapter 6

October 16, 1970, Gale and Brian were walking down the aisle. She was now nine months pregnant but was determined to be married before she had her baby. They were married at their family church. Gale wore an off yellow dress with a lace overlay that hung well past her feet, it was tight around her neck with a lace pattern between the neck and the chest. She wore a pair of white, flat patent leather shoes and her hair pinned up with a small bang. She made a beautiful bride, pregnant and all.

Brian wore a grey three-piece suit with a yellow shirt and a yellow and grey tie to match Gale's dress. There were two bride's maids, Cassandra and Ann. Trevon was the best man and two of his friends from the neighborhood were the groomsman. There were about forty to fifty people at the wedding. After the wedding they took pictures in the lobby of the church, where they ate afterwards, and everyone went home. Three weeks later, Gale and Brian gave birth to a six pound twelve-ounce little girl, who they named Regan.

*****

During the past six months everyone was so involved with Gale, her wedding and pregnancy that no one realized that Cassandra was beginning to pick up a little bit more weight than usual. She and Eric had been seriously dating for the past two years and she was now six and a half months pregnant. She did her best to avoid her parents as much as possible. She still worked at the convenient store, and when she wasn't at work she was across the street at Eric's, and when her parents would leave or when she saw they were no longer in the living room she would come home and go straight upstairs to James' old room, if it wasn't occupied. Her grandparents usually only went up there when it was their nap time or time to go to bed because Grandma Rose had bad knees and all those stairs did her no justice, and with it being fall, it was easy for Cassandra to put on a pair of jogging pants and a hoodie to hide her egg-shaped stomach.

The evening before Thanksgiving, Cassandra was helping her mother and grandmother prepare dinner for the next day. Gale and Brian were over, but they were in the living room with their baby and John was out with the boys doing what he did best, getting drunk.
"So, Cassandra, when is that baby due?" asked Grandma Rose.
"Huh?" Cassandra answered looking in a surprised manner.

"What you thought nobody knew? I noticed you trying to avoid the family and wear all those big clothes."

"It's cold."

"Baby, don't lie to your grandmother, there is not too much that goes on in this house that I don't know about, and you better believe that." Cassandra dropped her head and looked at the floor. Vivian didn't say too much, but she also noticed and so did John, but they weren't going to make her leave.

"So, what are you going to do with yourself?"

"What do you mean? Are you guys going to try to force me and Eric to get married as you did Gale?"

"No baby it's your life, you do whatever you feel is right."

"I appreciate that."

"So, when were you going to tell us? We've been waiting for the past two months."

"So, you knew?"

"Yes, but we wanted you to tell us."

"I'm sorry, Grandma I just didn't want you guys to be disappointed in me. I saw the way you guys were on Gale, and I didn't want that pressure and I really didn't want to deal with my dad."

"Well to be honest, your dad was the first one to notice. I had kind of thought, but then I said naw she wouldn't do that after what Gale just went through."

"What did dad say?"

"Nothing really, he just said, '*you know Cassandra is pregnant*' and he left the room."
"Wow, he wasn't angry?"
"No, but I hope you know that you and Eric will have to take care of your own baby. You and the baby can stay here since your Auntie Joyce and her kids moved out. Clifton and I will give you'll the whole attic to yourselves because we will probably be going back to Atlanta again soon and you and that baby can be comfortable and stay out of the way of your ole crazy daddy until you find your own place." Her grandparents had left and come back several times within the last couple of months just to make sure everything was alright. "Thanks guys." She hugged her mother and grandmother just as Gale walked through the kitchen with the baby. "Ugh, what's up with all this mushy hugging and stuff, don't ya'll see each other every day?"
"Well, Cassandra has some good news," said Vivian.
"What are you moving out of the country?" And she began to laugh. Cassandra rolled her eyes and decided to play her game with her. She was tired of her always being mean to her for no reason.
"Nope, actually I'm pregnant, and the baby and I will be staying up in the attic all by ourselves now that they got rid of you."
"Yeah right, first of all, who in the heck got you pregnant? I know it wasn't Eric's little fine

behind, or was it dad?" And Gale began to laugh.

"You are so fuckin' ignorant," yelled Cassandra with tears beginning to wail up in her eyes and grandma Rose smacked her upside her head.

"I'm sorry, Grandma, but that was uncalled for."

"What did she mean by that anyways?" asked Vivian.

"Mama, don't pay her any mind, she is just jealous." Vivian knew something was going on because John always let Cassandra get what she wanted, but treated Gale differently, but she was afraid of the truth and knew that if she confronted John, it would make matters worse for her. She was an old fashion Southern woman who didn't believe in divorce or a woman leaving her husband, no matter what the circumstances. She thought the less she knew the less guilty she would feel, and the things that she did know if she let it be, it might go away. "So ya'll gon' let her and that baby stay here, and ya'll made me and mine get out? Ever since we were little you let that brat get what she wanted. She got to go to modeling school, for free, but I had to pay my own way through college. She always got better clothes and stuff then me and she never had to do nothing that she didn't want to do like when we used to have to go all the way to Cleveland to clean all of that wood work for two dollars, I hated that mess and just because she decided to steal two extra dollars she didn't

have to do it any- more and now she can stay here with that baby. That is so messed up."
"Girl, stop living in the past, you are now married and ya'll seemed to be happy."
"Well make her get married like you did me."
Brian walked into the kitchen to find his wife crying. "What's going on in here?"
"Baby I told you that they didn't really care about me, and that Cassandra was their favorite."
"What do you mean, and why do you say that?"
"Cassandra is about to have a baby, and they are letting them live here but they made me leave."
"Well look at it like this, you left to be with me. Aren't you happy?"
"Yes, I am baby. I love you." Brian hugged his wife as he winked his eye at Vivian and Grandma Rose. He smiled at Cassandra. "Congratulations. When is the baby due?"
"February twenty eighth."
"So, they only gon' be like three months apart. What you having?"
"A girl."
"Ain't that sweet, two girls in three months, I sure hope they are closer than you two?"
"Yeah, that is sweet," said Vivian.
"Well, I wish you and Eric the best. Is he coming to dinner tomorrow?" asked Brian. Cassandra looked at her mother and grandmother for their approval.
  "He can come if he wants to. You know there will be plenty of food and he needs to get

to know the family better if he's going to be around." Cassandra smiled and Gale helped them finish preparing Thanksgiving dinner.

Chapter 7

"Oh my gosh, my stomach hurts so badly! Grandma, I think I'm going in labor. Can you take me to the hospital?" Cassandra cried as she slowly walked into the living room.
"Girl, you better stroll your little tail across that street and make Eric get his behind up and take you. If you're not home in the next hour, I'll call your mother, and we'll be there once she gets off work." Cassandra did as she was told, she looked out of the front door and didn't see his car, but she walked across the street anyways and his great aunt informed her that he was out for a while. She waddled back across the street and Grandma Rose called Vivian who rushed home from work. They arrived at the hospital and Cassandra was in labor for seven hours and right on her due date, February 28, 1970, at 6:32 a.m., she gave birth to a seven pound eight-ounce baby girl who could have easily been mistaken for a white child, that she named Darcella. Cassandra was so happy. They kept her baby in the nursery and she was at the window every other hour looking in at her baby. The nurses had to make her go to sleep because she did not want to leave her baby. Eric didn't come to the hospital because he claimed that he hated hospitals, but her mother and father were there every day to see their

granddaughter, and on the fourth day they all went home.

Life was a breeze the first couple of months. Cassandra had signed up for government assistance, so she had a check coming in every month and food stamps, plus she was babysitting for Eric's brother and his girlfriend, they had a three-year-old daughter who adored Cassandra. She didn't return to work at Seven Eleven but used her government check and her babysitting money to continue to help her parents with the bills and to supply all of her and her baby's needs. Her father made her buy her own food and that was all that she better eat. He was so petty that he would count the fruit and if something was missing, he was drilling Vivian, who always stood up for her daughter because to her that was just petty. Cassandra slept in until noon most days, since she had the attic to herself; she had a dorm room refrigerator in her room, so she really didn't have to go downstairs for much. Grandma Rose, who made sure she didn't have to get out of bed so that her body could heal properly, brought her all her meals in bed and made sure the baby had all her needs at her reach. Everyone loved Darcella so much she brought such joy to the family, and most of the time Cassandra's parents had Darcella downstairs in the living room with them spoiling their granddaughter.

Grandma Rose and Grandpa Clifton had gone back to Atlanta to take care of some business because they had decided to move to Ohio so they could be with their family. One afternoon Cassandra and Darcella were sitting on the couch; she was watching a movie and Darcella was snuggled in her arms. It was a hot day in the middle of July, the windows were open, and the fan was blowing, and they were enjoying the fresh air when she heard her father yelling at her mother.
"Bitch, you heard what the hell I just said!" She could barely hear her mother's soft voice, so she turned down the television set. The bedroom door opened, and she heard a lot of bumping. She laid Darcella on the couch and put a chair in front of it so she wouldn't roll onto the floor and went to see what all the commotion was, and when she walked around the corner, her father was choking her mother. Cassandra ran into the room and grabbed him off her.
"Get off of my mother! I'm tired of this shit!" John pushed Cassandra off his arm and Vivian picked up the clock radio and threw it at him and hit him in the back of the head.
"Get your lil' ass out of here before you get it next!" he yelled at Cassandra.
"This stuff has been going on for too long. Mom, aren't you tired of this mess? Why don't you just leave his ole' drunk ass? And I wish you would hit me. I am not a child anymore and that mess ain't gon' roll with me anymore."

"Cassandra baby why don't you and Darcella go across the street with her father for a little while?" asked Vivian.
"Mom, I'm not leaving you", and she began to cry. "You weren't doing this mess when Grandma and Grandpa were here because you know they would have put you in your place." John grabbed his switch blade off his nightstand and put it to Vivian's neck, he thought about what he was doing and realized it wasn't worth it and was about to put it away and accidently cut her on the shoulder.
"You crazy son of a bitch." Cassandra said softly as she slowly backed out of the room.
"Ya better go somewhere and mind your own damn business."
"My mother is my business. It's obvious that you don't give a damn about her, always putting your hands on her."
"You better shut the hell up before I put my hands on you."
"Hum." Cassandra began to smirk. "Haven't you done that enough?" John got off Vivian and went into the bathroom and stayed there for a good half an hour. Cassandra ran to the corner store and called the police and when the police arrived Vivian refused to press charges on him. Cassandra told the police about a lot of the beatings that had been going on, but without Vivian justifying it they wouldn't do anything. Once the police left, John told Cassandra she had to leave.

"Cassandra, I've been as patient as I could be with you. You don't work, you don't go to school, and you done had a baby. I've let you stay here even though you've violated every one of my rules, but since you want to be grown and all up in my business, it's time for you and your baby to go."

Cassandra looked at her mother with tear filled eyes. Vivian turned her head; she didn't know what to say.

"Fine I'll leave. Mama you can come with me. We can get a place toge...."

"Your mother's not going anywhere... just you."

Cassandra slowly walked out of the room and went into the living room to get her sleeping child. They went upstairs where she lies across her bed and fell asleep too. Cassandra didn't leave immediately because she really didn't have anywhere to go. She called her grandmother who suggested that she and the baby go and stay with Eric, but she didn't really want to do that because after she had the baby, he had become a little distant and controlling. Eric had moved out of his great aunt's house and into an apartment of his own on the other side of town.

    Several months had past and Cassandra was still in her parents' house, she tried her best to avoid her parents, especially her father, and when she did run into him, he always gave her an uncomfortable look and finally she decided to leave. John knew that Cassandra didn't have anywhere to go, and he was not going to put his daughter out on the street with a baby, but he figured if he continued to make her feel uncomfortable maybe she would go find her a place of her own. Cassandra told Eric what was going on at her parents' home and he welcomed her and his daughter, who was now almost eleven months and getting into everything, to live with him. He and his brother, who lived in the apartment upstairs from him, helped Cassandra move all their belongings, which wasn't a lot, to his apartment when her parents where both at work. Cassandra and Eric got along quite well, but he was so controlling and worked too much, he was trying to make sure that Cassandra and his daughter were comfortable.

 Cassandra, stuck in the house all day, would cook and clean up and was done within an hour or two, then she would lie around and watch television and that became boring. One afternoon, she had put Darcella down for a nap and was outside hanging up a flowerpot when a guy pulled up in a Ford Mustang, it wasn't all that nice, but he was nice looking.
"Hey, young thang. Do you need any help hanging up that pot?"
"No, I got it, thanks." And she smiled at him. The guy pulled his car to the curb and got out of the car.
"Are you sure, you look like you are struggling a little." The guy was about 5'11", a caramel

brown with an afro and he introduced himself as Charles. He helped her hang up her flowers and they talked for a few moments, and he left leaving her with his phone number. They would talk on the phone whenever she was bored, and he would come by periodically when Eric was at work and his nosey brother wasn't home and they would watch movies or just talk.

    About the third or fourth month that she and Eric lived together, Cassandra found out that she was three months pregnant. She stayed at home and played the role of a housewife but was still spending time with Charles. One night Eric was off from work and considering they didn't have a driveway; he always parked his car on the street and Charles had no clue as to what kind of car he drove. Charles came to Cassandra's bedroom window trying to surprise her, he tapped lightly, and she didn't come to the window, so he slowly raised the window and was about to climb in when the light came on. He smiled thinking it was Cassandra, but when he looked up, he saw a light skinned brother with a wife beater on and a pair of plaid pajama pants. He had never seen Eric and was in shock. He tried to jump down and run, but Eric had his 22mm in his hand and shot him in his leg. He fell to the ground but got up quickly and made it to his car. Cassandra continued to lay there acting scared and clueless, so Eric thought it was just an intruder. She never called or saw Charles again. Cassandra finally gave birth to her second child which was a little boy who she named Eric, Jr. He was eight pounds nine ounces, twenty-one inches long, with a head full of curly hair and the spitting image of his father. They all shared a one-bedroom apartment, which was fine since the kids were little but would have to think about a change for the future.

******

One afternoon Cassandra decided that she and the kids were going to go to the grocery store and hang out for a while. Cassandra got the kids dressed and then began to prepare herself. Eric was sitting in the living room and could see her walking back and forth from their bedroom to the bathroom. He saw her with her little jeans on and now a little make up, so he got up and went to the bathroom door.
"You need to do all of that just to go to the grocery store?"
"What? I'm just getting dressed."
"Who just wears little tight jeans and all that make up to the store? What you looking for, a man or something?"
"Don't you want your woman looking good?"
"Yeah for me, gon' ahead and go and hurry up and get back here." Cassandra untied her head scarf so that she could take out her curlers and comb her hair.

"What are you doing?"
"About to comb my hair."
"No, you can go just like that, you don't have to try to be all cute, or I can just take you myself."
"No thanks."
"Oh, and my brother told me that when you were working outside in the flowers the other day with those little bitty shorts on that guys were driving by blowing at you. The next time you go out there, you better put on some jogging pants or something. I've been around long enough to know what these men are about, and they only want one thing, believe me I know what's best for you." Eric always made comments insinuating that since he was much older, he knew more than she did. Cassandra grabbed her kids and put them both in the backseat. She couldn't believe he was making her go outside like this, she looked a mess. Ever since she had started dating, she made sure she always looked her best, and now it seemed as if she was going downhill.

*****

Cassandra had grown tired of sitting in the house all day with the kids, she loved them dearly but needed some grown up conversation and decided to go to Hammel College to major in Fashion Merchandising. This would give her an opportunity to travel and model in fashion shows. Eric wasn't too thrilled about her going out of town without him and the kids, but she didn't care. It gave her

the opportunity to be free and do what she always wanted to do. Her first trip was to New York City. She took her kids to her parents' neighbors, who had lived there since she was younger, they would sometimes help her with her kids if she needed a sitter and got on the bus with her classmates. She had the time of her life. She called Eric from her hotel room to let him know that she made it safely.
"Yeah, alright," he replied with no enthusiasm, and he ended the call. Cassandra was tired of him treating her like she was nothing and didn't have any feelings and decided when she came back, she was going to make a change.

    Monday morning started a new semester, and Cassandra was dropped off at school as she was everyday by Eric's brother. He didn't trust her to drive herself, he wanted to know where she was at all times. She entered her accounting class and she saw the man of her dreams. She felt as if she were in a movie, it was like everything froze and she couldn't see anyone but him, they made eye contact and they both smiled at each other. Cassandra was in a daze until she was interrupted by her professor.
"Excuse me ma' am. Can I help you?"
"Uh, hum? Oh… is this the accounting class?"
"You are at the right place." Cassandra took a seat next to Nathaniel and periodically glanced in his direction throughout the class. They talked as they walked to their next class, which

happed to be together, and by the end of the day he had given her his phone number.

Chapter 8

"Mama...Mama...Mom, I can't do this anymore." Vivian ran out of her bedroom to see who was yelling in her house like that at two in the morning. James came in late one night sweating and breathless.
"Boy, what are you doing here?"
"Mom, this is not a life for a human being. How could you guys let them keep me there?"
"Baby, we had no choice, they came and got you and said you had to go."
"Well, I'm not going back there, I don't care."
"How did you get here?"
"I told them that we had a family emergency, and they gave me two days, but I can't go back."
"If you go AWOL then you'll go to jail, and my heart can't handle that."
"I know mama, and I'm sorry."
"We'll work out something." After two weeks the General came looking for James, Vivian explained that this was not for her son. They made him return for a short time, and after a formal meeting with the General and the Sergeant, James was released from the military. The recruiter had lied and cheated to get James drafted to meet his quota. It turned into a he-said-she-said battle, and after being reevaluated James did not qualify and was let go. He moved back in with this his parents so

that he could get back on his feet. John wasn't too thrilled, but he had really missed his son.

    James and Eric had become close friends. Most days Eric would catch a ride to work with one of his coworkers or have James drop him off and allow him to keep the car, but he had to take Cassandra to school and to do her household shopping. James didn't mind because he was able to do whatever he wanted all day. James really didn't appreciate the way that Eric treated his sister, but he wasn't the type to interfere in anyone else's relationship. Since she was happy and willing to put up with his bull crap, he was going to stay out of it.

    Nathaniel and Cassandra couldn't talk as much as they wanted considering she lived with a controlling man, but every opportunity that she got she would call him, even if it was to talk for only five minutes while Eric was in the shower. She always remembered to dial her mother's phone number as soon as she hung up, just in case he decided to press the redial button. They had grown close and wanted a relationship but didn't know how to make it happen without someone getting hurt, so Cassandra started creeping around. "Look, James, I know that you and Eric are cool, but he treats me like crap, and although we got these kids together, I am so ready to move on."

"What you want me to do about it?"
"I don't know. I want to tell you something, but I want it to be between me and you."
"If it's something crazy that's going to get you in some trouble, I don't want to hear it." Cassandra shifted her body in the seat of the car.
"It is something crazy, but it's not going to get me in any trouble."
"Well, what's up?" Cassandra was now grinning from ear to ear. "Oh gosh."
"No listen." Cassandra said laughing. "I met this guy at my school, and I really like him. He is in a couple of my classes, we talk on the phone as much as possible, and I would rather be with him, but Eric is not trying to move on."
"You have to do whatever makes you happy, but you need to close one door before you open another."
"I know, but I want to at least start spending time with him."
"Well, there is no harm in having friends, you know a pimp like me, I got plenty of hoes," he said as he popped the collar of his shirt.
"We are not talking about your nasty ass."
They both began to laugh. "I'm serious though. Look we don't have classes tomorrow because the instructors are having a meeting." James looked at her while shaking his head. "Don't give me that look."
"Go head."

"Well can you take me to his house like you are taking me to school and then pick me up like you do every day?"

"Man don't try to get me caught up in your mess. Eric gives me his car everyday so that I can take care of my business, not for me to help you cheat on him."

"You are my brother, not his, and as long as you keep your mouth shut nobody will ever know."

"Man, we'll see." They pulled into her school parking lot.

"I'll be ready tomorrow at the same time. I love you." She kissed James on the cheek and hurriedly got out of the car.

Nathaniel and Cassandra began to spend a lot of time together, he would cook her lunch some days when they got out of classes early and have her back at the school before her ride was there to pick her up. She would find any excuse to get out of the house; she would take the kids to her sisters for a few hours and have Nathaniel's sister pick her up from around the corner. Their relationship started getting serious, and her feelings for Eric slowly faded away. She was to the point that she didn't care what he thought, and she told Nathaniel where she and Eric stayed and allowed him to pick her up from her house when Eric wasn't home. Eric had been tripping for way too long, and she was ready to move on.

James finally got a job on his own and was no longer able to take Cassandra to work so Eric would sometimes give her the car to go to school and she took full advantage of the opportunity to be with Nathaniel. He still stayed with his mother and five sisters, considering he was several years younger than Cassandra, so she would go over there, and if they were all home, they would go to hotels so they could be intimate.

Cassandra was usually out of school several hours before Eric got off work and would chill with Nathaniel until about forty-five minutes before Eric would get home, just enough time to get the kids and get dinner started.

One afternoon Cassandra had spent the afternoon with Nathaniel, and when she came outside to go home the car was gone. She was walking down the steps backwards while holding on to the banister just laughing and saying her goodbye's and when she turned around all she could do was close her eyes and shake her head. One of Nathaniel's neighbors was friends with Eric and saw him at the bar one night and they began to converse. "Man, I haven't seen you in a minute," said Eric.
"I always see your car over there on Stoner."
"I don't be on Stoner."
"Don't you still have that, Tan Cheval?"

"Yeah."
"Well, it be parked outside across the street from my house almost every day around two or three."
"Oh, really?" Eric asked with a distraught look on his face.
"Man, I'm not trying to get in your business or nothing but..."
"Oh, naw man you are cool. It was good seeing you." That Monday Eric went to work early and took a half of vacation day stating that he had a doctor's appointment, and considering he never called off or was even late, they had no problem with it. He had his brother pick him up and park the car on the next block where he could see his friend's house and waited for his car to pull up. At 2:27, he saw his car he shook his head in disbelief and waited for her to go into the house. He waited ten minutes and when she didn't come out, he had his brother drive him around the block. He took out his spare key and took the car home. An hour later Cassandra come out to leave and noticed the car missing her heart dropped to the pit of her stomach. She knew it hadn't been stolen because there was no glass on the ground, and she always locked the doors. She asked one of Nathaniel's sisters to give her a ride to pick up her children and then to take her home, and when she got there the car was parked in front of the house. She hesitantly got out of the car, got the kids out, and saw Eric standing

in the window. Luckily it was a nice day and Eric's sister had the window rolled halfway down and was waving goodbye to Cassandra. When she got into the house, she tried to act nonchalant and put all the blame on Eric.
"Why did you come get the car?"
"Why the fuck weren't you at school?"
"I had a little extra time, so I decided to visit one of my friends while I waited for the kids to get out of school."
"That's not what you are supposed to be doing. That's why I don' let you do shit. You could have had dinner ready and everything else. I swear you get on my damn nerves." This time Eric didn't jump on her. He was tired of her games but wanted to be there for his kids. Cassandra was no longer allowed to drive the car to school.

One day Cassandra had gotten out of school early. She called her parent's house looking for James, but he was nowhere to be found. She called Eric, but he was still at work, so she had Nathaniel give her a ride downtown where she caught the bus the rest of the way home. She was home later than normal, and Eric had already picked up the kids, and as soon as she walked in the door, Eric slapped her in the mouth.
"Where the fuck have you been?"
"I had to catch the bus because our classes were over early, and I didn't have a ride home."

"Bull shit!" he said as he choked her, and she fell backwards onto the couch. "You were out with your little boyfriend, and that's why you always tryin' to find an excuse to get out of here."
"What the hell are you talking about? I was at school like I said. If you would let me drive myself, I wouldn't have this problem."
"You are not responsible enough. That will just give you time to go lay-up with somebody else and be home before I get here to freshen up, and I don't need the extra stress. You see what happened before, I don't believe that you were going to see your home girl every day, but I'm not going to dwell on it."
"Well, I see we have a lot of trust issues here." He slapped her again.
"Because you don't know how to sit your hot ass down, always wearing those tight jeans and tank tops putting on all that make up just to go to school."
"This is how I dressed when we met."
"Yeah, and you were looking for a man then, but you have one now and you don't need to look good for nobody but me." This had been going on since they had moved in together and didn't look as if it was going to stop any time soon. Cassandra was tired of it.

*****

Cassandra's cousin, Dan, was having problems at home and was welcomed to move in with Cassandra and her family so that he could finish school. Cassandra had a big heart and couldn't see any one in her family being homeless. Dan was a senior in high school, and they were close to the school, so it was convenient.

Eric started stressing about the kids growing and needing more things, about the bills going up, and about not having any extra money because they had an extra mouth to feed. Cassandra wasn't babysitting as much as she used to because Eric's brother's kids had started school and didn't need a babysitter as much so Cassandra decided to get a night job at a convenient store working eleven at night to seven in the morning not too far from home where she could walk if needed and with Dan being there, he was able to watch the kids at night and wake them up in the morning and give them breakfast so they wouldn't be late for school. Cassandra's job didn't pay much, but it was something to do, and it put extra money in her pocket. Cassandra's attitude had changed, and she no longer paid Eric any attention, so he automatically assumed that it was another man. He would pop up at her job sometimes with the kids just to check on her sometimes more than once a night. He would come up to the school and pick her up when she was expecting James or Eric's brother who sometimes picked her up to be there just to see if she was talking to someone. One day she and one of her professors were talking in the parking lot, and Eric sat there and watched them. He saw her writing down some information in her notebook and became instantly pissed. As soon as she got into the car, he started slapping her around and accusing her of cheating. He snatched her notebook and started flipping through the pages only to find a list of reference books to help her with one of her assignments. He didn't care, and eventually she dropped out of school.

Chapter 9

A whole year had passed, and Nathaniel and Cassandra were happily in a relationship. He hated the fact that Cassandra had dropped out of school and tried his best to convince her to go back, but she just couldn't deal with Eric's lack of trust and insecurity, and she didn't want him to ever catch her talking with Nathaniel. She would take vacations at the convenient store, and she and Nathaniel would spend most of the day together at her house while Eric was at work. Nathaniel knew that Eric and Cassandra lived together, but he figured if she allowed him to come over there then their relationship must not be that solid. If she didn't care, why should he? But most days she would catch a cab to Nathaniel's mother's house or have his sister pick her up after Eric dropped her off. She would go into the store and buy a Pepsi and a bag of chips, and once he left, she would check out and go to a pay phone and call her ride.

******

One morning Cassandra was getting ready for work and was brushing her teeth and became instantly sick. *"Maybe I'm coming down with a virus or something,"* she thought. She got to work and began to throw up again,

and this happened every day for the next two weeks. Eric noticed and automatically assumed that she was pregnant again, and this made him happy because he figured that a new baby would bring them closer and maybe help their relationship. Eric came home from work with a dozen roses and handed them to his sleeping woman.
"Get up baby let's go get something to eat."
"I'm tired. I don't really feel like going anywhere."
"Come on, we need to go celebrate."
"Celebrate what?"
"Our new baby."
"Boy, please, ain't nobody having no baby."
"I've been noticing you getting sick every morning, and I see you sleeping a lot lately, and you're picking up weight. Something is going on."
"It's probably just stress from work. I'm just tired." Eric didn't believe that. He knew Cassandra and she wasn't going to lose her nice figure because of a job. She would work out so that she could stay slim.
"Are you coming or what?"
"Naw, not today, maybe next time."
"This the shit I be talking about, you always say that I don't take you nowhere or do nothing with you, and then when I ask you always turn me down." He took two fingers and pushed her forehead. Cassandra didn't feel like fighting with him, so she rolled over and went back to sleep.

Eric had begun drinking a lot and the abuse just got worse, physically and mentally, Cassandra grew tired and decided that she was going to move out, but she didn't know how without having to fight with Eric. Cassandra worked as many hours as she could for the next four weeks and began looking for an apartment for her and her kids. She had gone to the doctors, and she was two months pregnant, and she knew that it was Nathaniel's, and that Eric would kill her if he found out she had been talking to another man let alone sleeping with one. Cassandra finally had saved up enough money for a down payment and had found a place to go. She had gotten a moving truck with movers that said they could have her moved out in two to three hours, plenty enough time to be gone before Eric got off work. The movers had the truck halfway loaded when Eric pulled up. His brother had called and told him that she was moving out. He made the movers put all her stuff back, he paid them and, of course, jumped on her when they left.
"Oh, that's how the fuck you doing things these days? You just gone up and leave and take my kids without saying nothing?" He smacked her.
"You are just like my father and that's why I'm leaving. I hate you and I hate living here. I am extremely unhappy, and I've been telling you that for the past couple of months, but instead of trying to make things right with me, all you

do is put me down and abuse me. I can't live like this, and I'm not going to let my kids see you put me through this."

"Cassandra, I love you and my kids, and I don't want ya'll to go. I know I don't always show you or tell ya'll, but I do, and I'll do whatever it takes to make you stay."

"You can start by not putting your hands on me."

"Is that all it takes to get you to stay? So, what's going on with my child, is it a boy or girl?" he asked as he rubbed her pouch of a stomach.

"I don't know yet."

"When were you going to tell me?"

"When the time was right, we just haven't been getting along really well and I just thought that it would just make things worse." She knew it wasn't his and she didn't plan on ever telling him, she was just going to leave and never come back.

"I'm going to make things better, I promise." Eric left and went to the bar and Cassandra called Nathaniel and talked to him until she fell asleep on the phone. Cassandra stayed with Eric and finally gave birth to her eight pounds nine ounces little girl whom she named Jasmine. One of her neighbors had to take her to the hospital and watched over the kids until Eric was home because she called Eric and he wasn't willing to leave work. She was so upset because no one came to visit her in the hospital, and she was all alone. She didn't understand what was going on with her life, she wanted to be happy, but she was miserable. Eric knew that she was in the hospital, and she couldn't understand why he wasn't there. They had their share of problems, but all relationships did. She understood why Nathaniel wasn't there, and she was fine with that because she didn't know if Eric would just pop up and she didn't want to get caught up, not just yet.

Chapter 10

Cassandra was finally released from the hospital, she felt well rested and went back home to her unhappy family. She had missed her other children and was glad to be back in their presence. She was off work for several weeks. She had taken the older kids to school and was about to get started on dinner and decided to go upstairs and check on Jasmine, and there was a garden snake crawling on her! She ran into the bedroom and snatched her out of the bed screaming at the top of her lungs. "Oh Jesus, help my baby. Why is this happening to me? Oh, Lord." Cassandra ran downstairs and sat on the couch where she stayed until Eric came home from work.
"You didn't cook dinner today, woman?"
"No, I didn't, I was getting it ready and went to check on Jasmine and there was a snake crawling on her. I can't deal with this! The kids and I are leaving until you get a better place." Cassandra called her mother in tears and told her what had happed and informed her that she and the kids were coming to stay with them, and Vivian assured her that it would be alright. They stayed there for a little over two months and then Eric had gotten another house with three bedrooms, and they moved back in with him, but this time things were worse. He would beat her up all the time and

most nights he didn't come home. She wanted to leave but still didn't have anywhere to go and she didn't like staying with her parents because her father fussed and complained about everything the kids did and she couldn't live like that, and the kids were happy with their father. She continued to work at the convenient store, but only part time, and decided to find something else to do because she hated being at home as much as she was, so she decided to find another job. She was hired at Ohio Bell, a phone company, where she worked thirty-five hours a week. She worked both jobs, and in her spare time she was with Nathaniel. On her off days she wouldn't tell Eric and would still have him drop her off, she would go into the front door, go to the cafeteria and call a cab and then go out the back door. Eric had called her job several times, and they told him that she wasn't there. When he asked her about it, she always had an excuse like she was in the bathroom and maybe they thought that she left, or she took a late lunch and had rode to McDonald's with a coworker. He didn't believe her, but what could he say? The next time he called her job and they said she wasn't there and he knew he had dropped her off, he left work and went to her job, he couldn't get to her office because it was an unauthorized area for customers, so he pulled his car to the back of the building where all of the business trucks were where he could see both sides of the building and parked. One

hour later Cassandra was pulling up in her cab and saw his car just as they were also pulling into the back of the building, she had the cab driver go all the way around the parking lot and back to the front as she sloped down in the back seat, she didn't go back into the building because he would have seen her so she just sat on the wall a couple feet from the door where Eric couldn't see her and five minutes later he circled around to pick her up.
"Why the hell are you sitting out here and not in that building like you always are?"
"Because I wanted to sit down, my feet hurt in these clogs."
"Yeah, I bet. So, was that you in that cab that I saw circling the building?" Cassandra's heart began to race.
"What cab?" Eric smacked his lips.
"Never mind." He didn't want her to know that he was spying on her because next time he was going to catch her.

****

One evening Cassandra had prepared dinner and was waiting for Eric to come home from work so that they could eat dinner, and by 7:30 she grew tired of waiting. Her kids had a bedtime which was 8:30, so they ate without him. She went to work that evening, asking the neighbor to keep an eye on the kids, and when she came home the next morning there was no sign of him being there. She took a short nap and then got ready for her second job. When he still hadn't returned, she called off and waited for his return. He came home that afternoon, and they got into a big argument because she was tired of everything. She knew that she wasn't doing the right thing and it made no sense for them both to be doing wrong, two wrongs don't make a right, so she confronted him about his whereabouts the night before.

"So where were you all night?"

"Working." He answered without even looking at her."

"Working who because you sure as hell wasn't at your nine to five."

"Look I'm tired and I'm about to go to bed."

"You are a sorry low life mother fucker, and I hope like hell your…" They were interrupted by a knock at the door.

"Eric Holmes?" Cassandra sat down on the couch as Eric opened the door. There stood a short Caucasian man with a neatly trimmed beard.

"Yes?" He asked with a questioning look on his face.

"Do you own a Tan Cheval?"

"Yes. Why?"

"There is some lady up on the highway, and the car is broken down. I stopped to help her, and she asked me to come down here to get you to assist her." He turned around and looked back at Cassandra, who was sitting on the couch holding her baby, and just walked out of the door following the man. Cassandra

watched out of the window for a few seconds and then followed him to the highway. By the time she walked up the hill and reached the highway she was out of breath and found Eric and a small-framed, light-skinned woman that stood about five foot two inches with long jet-black hair laying on her shoulders standing in front of his car with the hood up. Cassandra walked over to the car and cleared her throat. Eric turned around and just looked at her like what are you doing here?
"Eric?"
"Baby, look in the glove compartment and grab my gun." Eric said as he watched Cassandra, he knew she was good for acting crazy and making a scene and he wasn't in the mood. Cassandra couldn't believe that he was playing her like this. The lady walked to the car to look for the gun, and Cassandra and Jasmine slowly walked home. She was hurt. Although she was doing him wrong, she didn't think that he would do her like this, he actually asked another woman to pull a gun on the mother of his children. Cassandra walked in the unlocked door crying as hard as she could. She saw Eric's leather jacket lying on the couch, she grabbed the jacket, turned on the eye on the stove, and threw the leather jacket on the stove. When it started to burn, she and the baby got into the coat closet. Eric came home and looked through the window and the kitchen was so smoky that he could hardly see. He called the fire department from a neighbor's

house and then busted out the window and climbed into the house he removed the burning jacket, threw it on the floor and stomped out the fire. He found Cassandra and Jasmine in the closet cradled on the floor. The fire department arrived and the only thing that was burned was the oven, and there was black soot on the walls and ceiling. Cassandra left and went to stay with her parents for a couple of days, but things were worse there then they were at home. Her parents weren't happy with her continuing to leave Eric and then go back. Her father, as always, had something to say about any mess that the kids made, and they were living too far away from the kids' school and her job, so she went back. Cassandra was miserable. Things had gotten so bad between the two of them, and she didn't know what else to do. They argued all the time about every little thing, and they would say mean things to each other that would make the other one want to jump on the other one. Every time they had sex she felt as if she was being raped all over again because she didn't want to be there and was afraid of him. This wasn't love, the love that she felt and desired was with Nathaniel. One evening they were having one of their arguments and things got out of hand.

"I hate you, you sorry bastard, and that's why I'm never here. I'm going to find me a good man, and me and my kids are going to be happy. You can go ahead with that little white-looking bitch and be happy," yelled Cassandra.

"You can get the fuck, out but you are leaving my kids and we will probably be better off without you here."

"I wouldn't leave my kids here with you if I was in my grave. Your sorry ass can't even take care of yourself, and when we do leave don't be mad when my kids are calling another man daddy." Eric slapped her in the mouth. Cassandra smacked him back, he threw her onto the couch, grabbed his coat and left. He went to the bar and got completely wasted. When he came home that evening and beat Cassandra giving her a concussion. She didn't love him anymore and was ready to get out of the relationship and be with Nathaniel. She went to the hospital and gave a police report. Eric was arrested. When the police arrived at their home, they handcuffed him, put him in the back of the car. She closed the door to her home and locked it feeling relieved, then she looked out the window and gave him a finger and he went to jail. The court day was scheduled for three days after he was released from jail, Cassandra pressed charges on him, and he was told he had to leave his house until they went to court. On the day they went to court, Cassandra told them that she was afraid to stand by him in the court room and told the judge that if he ever put his hands on her again that she would scald him with boiling water. The police looked at their past records and saw that there were several police reports for domestic violence and told Eric that he had to

find someplace else to stay since she had the kids, and it was just him. Someone else had to go to the house and pick up his things because he was not allowed back there. He was ordered to pay her child support and her rent. The first two months she was receiving her payments as ordered, but one evening he was on the highway and must have looked at the house to see if there was any activity there when he saw a blue car in the driveway. He decided to come over to pay her the child support. He blew the horn, and she looked out and saw it was him and went outside.
"What are you doing here?"
"I was just dropping off your money for this month. Whose car is that?"
"Why?"
"Because I asked you a question. I know you don't have nobody in *my* house around *my* kids."
"You are tripping." Eric got out of the car and pushed past Cassandra and ran into the house, and Nathaniel was sitting on the couch right by the door watching television. Eric flipped out.
"What the fuck are you doing here in my house?" Nathaniel looked around.
"Who are you talking to? Last I checked this was Cassandra's house.
"Oh, you wanna get smart. You must be the mofo' that was sleeping with my woman when we were together because I know she was acting all brand new for some reason."

"Well, if I was, then that mean you must not have been doing something right, so I would advise you to do whatever you came here to do and go on about your business." By this time the kids were standing at the top of the steps watching.

"Eric what do you want?"

"I came to pay my child support, but I see that you've moved on real quick so if this is what you want then let that mofo' take care of you and your kids."

"You are acting real ignorant right now, and I'd advise you to give me my money and leave."

"Fuck you, bitch, I ain't giving you nothing."

"Watch your mouth around these kids. That is so disrespectful," said Nathaniel.

"Mind your fucking business." Eric started walking out of the door then he stopped and turned around and looked at Nathaniel. Nathaniel saw him out of his peripheral vision ignoring him but staying alert. Eric swung a right-hand punch at the back of Nathaniel's head. He ducked as he jumped off the couch. Cassandra was pushed back out the door. Eric, unaware that Nathaniel knew karate, stood up and was hit in the eye. They tussled in the living room in front of the kids until Nathaniel did a move and hurt Eric's wrist. Cassandra couldn't see what was going on because they were in front of the door, but she knew it wasn't good. She finally got into the house, and they stopped. They both had to go to the hospital, Eric for a fractured wrist and

Nathaniel for a broken blood vessel in his eye. Cassandra felt terrible and didn't want to live her life like this. She went to the courthouse and got a restraining order put on Eric, and since he wasn't allowed to come to his own house, he refused to pay the bills and his child support. *"Is this real love, fighting, lying and stalking. What did I do to deserve this?"* Cassandra thought. She hated herself and the fact that she was ever born. She filed for a divorce because they were together so long the marriage was considered a common law marriage.

    One morning Cassandra had overslept because the night before she and Eric had argued half the night, and since she didn't have a car, she was going to be late for work unless she could find a ride. She quickly dressed her three children and took them to the neighborhood day care where she had enrolled them when she was first hired at Ohio Bell. She called her parents to see if her brother was there, but he wasn't so she called a cab and was fifteen minutes late. She tried to sneak into her office, but her supervisor saw her and called her into her office.
"Oh, Cassandra, I see you're running a little late today."
"Yeah, I overslept. I apologize, it won't happen again."
"Yeah, it better not or you will be looking for another job." Cassandra gave her snooty boss

a distraught look this was her first time being late, so she didn't understand why she was tripping like this.
"Alright, I will try not to let it happen again." Cassandra turned around and rolled her eyes as she walked out of her office. When she got to her desk there was a slim Caucasian woman with glasses on the end of her nose sitting there on her phone.
"Excuse me, why are you in my seat?" The lady covered the receiver of the phone.
"Well since you weren't here at your start time, I figured you weren't coming today. It is a Friday, and you know how you people like to have a long weekend." Cassandra was not in the mood for this racist crap today.
"What the hell do you mean by 'you people'? For all you know I could have been scheduled to be late." The lady ended her call and turned to face Cassandra.
"Well, you weren't because I went and asked the supervisor where you were, and boy am I glad I did because she didn't even know you weren't here."
"So, you snitched on me?"
"If that's what you guys call it, I was just inquiring, if you know what that means."
"Get your stuck-up ass out of my seat before I make you. I am not in the mood for this mess."
"Oh my, please watch your language, you are in a place of business."
"I don't give a damn where I am, you are not going to keep making these racist comments."

"What are you going to do if I do? I will have a talk with Mr. Smiles, and you will be looking for another job."
"Yeah, I know your nasty ass be in there sucking his dick on your lunch breaks that's the only way you get promotions." The lady grabbed her mouth in shock.
"Don't sit there acting like I'm lying." The lady turned beet red. "That's why your breath smell like that with your nasty ass." The lady got up and charged at Cassandra with a pencil and stabbed her in the neck, it made a small puncture and only bled a small amount, but she went to the hospital anyways just to make sure she didn't have lead poisoning.

 Cassandra took a leave from Ohio Bell because she couldn't deal with all that stress, and they weren't giving her many hours at the convenient store so she couldn't afford all of the bills. She came home from work one day and there was a notice from the sheriff stating that she had to move out. What was she going to do? She had three kids that she was responsible for, she just wanted to lie down and die but she couldn't, she had to stay strong for her kids. She started receiving a lot of collection calls and notices and decided to apply for Section 8 to receive low-income housing. Two weeks later she had a voucher for section 8 housing, it wasn't really what she wanted but it was a roof over their heads, and they were warm and didn't have to worry about rent, but it didn't feel like home. She stayed there for one year but couldn't deal with the mice and the house's condition. She got rid of the mice and fixed it up real nice, but it just wasn't what she was looking for. Cassandra moved into a different house, but she didn't like the neighborhood. She had met a new male friend that she fell in love with because she was lonely. Nathaniel had been distant ever since the fight with Eric.

    One morning Cassandra woke up in a great mood, she got to work fifteen minutes early, talked with the other workers, got set up, and clocked in. It was two weeks before Easter, and she was going to help decorate the store between customers. They had the music playing in the back room so it could be heard in the store, and she was singing along to an old tune. She was up on the ladder hanging a large crochet egg over the cooler when the ladder moved, and she fell onto an ice cream cooler. She lay there for several minutes before she realized what happened, and when she tried to get up her body hurt like hell. One of her coworkers ran to see if she was alright. "Oh my gosh, Cassandra. Are you alright?" "No, call the ambulance my body feels numb." The worker did as she was instructed and five minutes later Cassandra was being taking away in the back of an ambulance. She had severe back injuries and was off on Workers Compensation. She was off for quite some time and decided to take a settlement and was no longer able to work for the convenient store. Cassandra was out of work for several years being a stay-at-home mom she received a government check, a utility check and food stamps to help take care of her family. Time went by, the kids were all in school, and she became bored sitting at home by herself and decided to look for a job. Cassandra had looked but didn't see anything that interested her, and one afternoon she was at Dr. Lando's office for an appointment for her back and was making small talk and mentioned that she was looking for a job and wouldn't you know, he was looking for a housekeeper. Cassandra knew how to keep a house and figured this would be easy money. She took the job and was to start the next Monday.

    Cassandra arrived at Dr. Lando's immaculate house which consisted of three bedrooms, a large bathroom, beautiful dining room/living room with built in bookshelves that contained shelves of medical books and a finished basement. Cassandra was impressed. Dr. Lando went over all her expected duties, which mainly included washing dishes, doing laundry, cooking dinner, making the beds, running the sweeper and keeping the bathroom clean and then he introduced her to his wife who was disabled and who she would also care for. The first week went excellent and she and Mrs. Lando

got along great, but when she became comfortable with her, she turned into a slave driver. Mrs. Lando had a bell that she kept beside her bed and what seemed like every ten minutes she would ring that bell for something, it could be a glass of water, a cut apple, a book to read or just to fluff her pillow, and she did it because she needed the money and was being paid under the table and could still receive all her benefits. Cassandra worked with this family for about a year and had become disgusted with them letting the dog eat with them and out of their dishes and Mrs. Lando purposely making a mess so that Cassandra could clean it up. One day Cassandra was getting ready to go home after doing all of her expected chores when she heard Mrs. Lando call her from the back room.
"Cassandra."
"Yes ma'am?"
"I know you are not leaving."
"I have completed all of my chores so yes I am leaving." She looked up and saw Mrs. Lando was creeping around the corner.
"Well, I see that my little doggie, Squeakers, has made a little pooh, pooh mess."
"Okay…"
"Go clean it up!"
"I'm sorry Mrs. Lando, but I don't clean up after no dog. That's not part of my responsibility."
"Well, you either clean it up or you will not get paid for today."

"Like hell I won't! I have done everything that Mr. Lando had asked me to do and he never mentioned anything about no dog."
"Well, I make the rules around here, and I say go clean it up."
"I'm not."
"Alright, then go ahead and leave. I'll see you next week."
"Can I have my pay now?"
"I just told you that if you didn't clean up that mess you weren't getting paid, did you think that I was playing, because I wasn't."
"No disrespect, Mrs. Lando, but don't make me whip your ass over my money disabled or not."
"Are you threatening me?"
"No, I'm just telling you facts."
"Get out of my house and don't come back!"
"Oh, I didn't plan on coming back, but I would appreciate my pay before I leave."
Just as Cassandra was about to leave Mr. Lando walked in the door, Cassandra explained everything that was going on to him, and of course he paid her, but she still quit. Now she was back to being unemployed and depending just on the government.

Chapter 11

A month had past, and Cassandra didn't know what she was going to do about money, if she got a job, she would lose her benefits and her rent would go up, and she really couldn't afford that right now. One afternoon, she was sitting at home watching 'Lavern and Shirley' when her phone rang. She was hesitant about answering it, thinking it may have been another bill collector, but she said, *'to hell with it'* and answered and was glad that she did. It was Mr. Lando.
"Hello, Cassandra?"
"Yeah, who is this?"
"It's Mr. Lando."
"What's the problem?"
"There's no problem, well not really."
"I'm listening."
"Well…" He paused, "we can't find anyone who works as well as you and…" A smile grew upon her face.
"Okay."
"Do you want your job back?"
"Look, I can't deal with your crazy wife."
"She promised that she would let you do your job without any interruptions."
"What about that dog?"
"That's not part of your job, and you don't have to worry about that."
"When do you want me to start back?"

"In the morning, if you can."
"I'll be there at my normal time."
"Oh, Mrs. Lando is going to be ecstatic."
"I bet, see you tomorrow and thanks."
Cassandra worked with Mrs. Lando for a whole month, and just grew tired of that kind of work. She wanted a real job. The money was good, and he paid her under the table, but it just wasn't worth it anymore. The following morning, she went to work did what she had to do, and that evening she left and never came back.

    They say an idle mind is the devil's workshop and sitting at home all day doing nothing kept Cassandra's mind going. She was lonely and beginning to think about Nathaniel, a lot. She finally realized that she was in love with him and was afraid because as a child she never had the love that a child should have, and all she ever wanted was to be loved, she wanted her father to love her like a little girl should be loved. She wanted him to tuck her in at night and tell her good night. She wanted him to put a bandage on her knee if she fell, but instead he raped her repeatedly. She never thought that anyone would love her for who she is, except her kids. She and Nathaniel would spend time together, sometimes, but he was a ladies' man and had too many other women in his life. Cassandra knew he had a steady girlfriend that he played volleyball with, but she didn't care. She wanted him and planned on making him hers. She wanted so badly for him to marry her. She put up with being second place for quite some time, but every time she thought of him being with another girl, she felt dirty all over again. She would have frequent flashbacks about what her father had done to her, and that made her never want to be alone. To occupy her time, Cassandra began to see a guy named Gerald. He wasn't exactly what she was looking for, but he kept coming around, calling and doing whatever he could to get her attention, so she let down her guard. But in the back of her mind Nathaniel was who she really wanted. Gerald had a decent job and was able to help her financially, if needed, so she kept him around, she didn't want her kids to have to struggle and go through what she went through, she wanted them to be happy.

Although Cassandra was chasing Nathaniel, she still put a lot of focus on her kids and made sure they stayed in school. She was depressed a lot but knowing that her kids loved her, and she could love them back gave her strength, she sat down and reevaluated her situation and decided from that day forward her kids would come first, well after God of course, and if she had grandchildren they would be like her own children.

Chapter 12

Cassandra tried working at hotels, but they were too hard. Her life was so messed up, she wished she could have stayed at home with her parents, but she couldn't see that happening because of her father. She tried working odd jobs here and there, but it was too hard with raising three kids on her own with no car or bus fair to even get her back and forth until she received her first paycheck after working two weeks in the hole. Once she added everything up with the decrease in her government benefits, she was better off sitting at home.

With everything going on with Cassandra she didn't realize that her now fourteen-year-old daughter, Darcella, was pregnant until she had a miscarriage. Cassandra was shocked and upset, she didn't allow her daughter to date, but she did allow her male friends to come over and visit because she knew that kids are going to be kids and if it was something that they really wanted to do they were going to find a way, so she figured if she allowed the boys to come over at least she could supervise them. She didn't chastise Darcella or say anything negative to her, but she did assure her that she really wanted her to finish school and that a baby is a big responsibility. One year later Darcella became pregnant again by the same guy with her first daughter, Cheryl. Cassandra wasn't surprised but wasn't ready to be a grandmother either. She kept wondering how she was going to take care of another child. Darcella and her baby's father got along well, and he was there for the most part, but a year or so later he got another girl pregnant. Her parents made them get married, then he left and went to the Army, so Cassandra helped raise her granddaughter. Darcella did continue to go to school, they had a maternity school that allowed the parents to bring their children to school so they would have no excuse as to why they didn't graduate. The school wasn't close to home, so she and her child had to catch the bus every day, but she had no problem doing that. If Cheryl was sick or something, Cassandra would allow Darcella to leave her at home with her because she really loved her grandbaby and she spoiled her to death, but she also wanted Darcella to learn some responsibility. The birth of Cheryl changed Cassandra's life, she now felt that she had someone that needed her and would love her back and this changed her life. She knew that her kids loved her, too, but they were older and doing their own things. The girls were usually with their friends, and Eric Jr. was into sports and that's all he cared about. He did boy things like trying to do stunts on his bike, and fell off and broke his arm, but he continued to ride and play sports even with his injuries.

The following year Jasmine, at the age of fourteen, became pregnant by her boyfriend. She didn't try to hide it, but she didn't tell her mother either until she was asked, and several months later she gave birth to her son, Dominic. Cassandra became depressed and stayed in the bed, she felt as if she was the blame for her children getting pregnant, and to make matters worse, seven months later Darcella had another baby girl who she named Kim. Now Cassandra felt as if she was just being punished, but later realized that she did nothing wrong. She was the one that had been hurt, she never had any guidance and had to learn on her own. Her mother tried to help, and her father tried to give her advice, but how can you trust someone who has raped you and didn't protect you?

Cassandra didn't expect her daughters to try to take all those kids to school on the bus, so she kept her grandchildren and allowed them to go back to public schools with their friends. Cassandra then became tired because a newborn, an infant, and a toddler is a lot for one person, so she made her daughters take the kids to daycare, which was in walking distance, every morning before they went to school. This lasted through the fall and then the weather started getting bad, and being a loving grandparent, Cassandra was tired of the kids getting sick from having to be out in that cold, so she began to keep them again and became attached like they were her own. This did interfere with her relationship with Nathaniel, but she wasn't happy anyways, so she started looking for love from another man which only caused more problems with her boyfriend. The kids kept her occupied, but she needed some grown up time and a companion. Darcella became pregnant with her third child just as she was about to graduate from high school, now this was becoming too much for Cassandra, she couldn't even think straight anymore. She couldn't take care of all these babies. She tried, but it was too hard, and she had to find some help, so she went to children services, explained their situation, and was given a part time nanny who came to their home three days a week to help take care of the kids so that Darcella could finish school. Cassandra was lost and didn't know what to do, she felt as if she was going to have a mental break down, but she knew that her kids needed her and so did her grandchildren, so she had to stay strong for them.

    Eric Jr. had graduated from high school during all of this and had received a football scholarship out of state and was gone before he turned eighteen. Cassandra knew that with all he'd been through, all he'd had to put up with, having to give up his bedroom and take the basement so that his sisters and their children could all be in the same rooms, and having to help with his nieces and nephews, hearing them cry all night while he was trying to sleep, he deserved this, and she knew he was going to do something with himself. She was so proud of her son because he was able to play in the All-Star games before he went to college and was announced the player of the year in high school. Things were hard for her children, but they all still managed to graduate. Their father bought some of their school clothes, and she did what she could. They didn't have a lot, and sometimes their clothes would get too small, but that was all that they had so they had to make do. Cassandra did try to work, but she was always stressed and began to get migraines so badly that she couldn't work a lot. Her kids tried to take care of her because they felt sorry for her, but they were still kids with kids. Her parents had moved down the street from her because they were getting of age, and James had become ill. Cassandra stayed in the bed, sometimes three to four days out of the week, and was in and out of the hospital a lot for her headaches. Sometimes she felt like dying because the headaches were so painful that she couldn't take care of her kids or grandkids. They would look at her fearful that something would happen to her, and they would be alone. They never fought, argued or did anything in front of their mother that would stress her out more. They were home alone a lot while she was in the hospital, but they did what they were expected to do and took care of each other, and the house was always like it was supposed to be when she returned. Cassandra was placed on disability and a few months later started receiving a check every month and no longer had to worry about going to work or how she was going to pay her bills.

Chapter 13

One afternoon Cassandra was at home cleaning, and someone from the neighborhood came running down the street and began to bang on her door.
"Cassandra, Cassandra!" the lady yelled. Cassandra came to the door with her head scarf on, a pair of sweatpants and an old t-shirt.
"Damn girl, why the hell you yelling my name like that? What's wrong with you?"
"I'm sorry." She said trying to catch her breath. "It's your father; he's lying on the ground. I don't know what's wrong with him. Come on!"
They both ran out of the house, Cassandra didn't even close her door, and ran up the street. When they reached her father, there were two strange men helping him into the house, they laid him on the couch, and it didn't look good. Cassandra called 9-1-1 and then her mother at work. She ran home, locked up her house, grabbed her keys and was back before the ambulance arrived. The ambulance pulled up and worked on James as some other paramedics talked to the guys that had helped him. They put him in the back of the ambulance and rushed off, and Cassandra followed behind them in her parents' car. Cassandra was watching the window of the ambulance and saw her father rise, and she

could see his face and it looked to say, '*I'm sorry*'. When they arrived at the hospital, they took James to the back. Cassandra called Gale and informed her as to what was going on and went to pick her mother up from work. They returned to the hospital and sat there for several hours, and Cassandra grew impatient and decided she was going to go home and put on some more decent clothes. She took a hot shower to relieve some stress, put on a pair of jeans and a t-shirt and was on her way back to the hospital when her house phone rang.
"Hello?"
"Cassandra?"
"Yes?"
"Are you on your way back to the hospital?" It was Gale.
"Yeah. Why?" There was a brief silence.
"Dad died." Cassandra grabbed her chest as she hung up the phone and fell back onto the couch. After about five or ten minutes she regained her strength and went back to the hospital. When she returned all the family was there. They let his mom, kids, brother and sisters all come in to say good-bye. Cassandra pulled the sheet back and saw that his chest had been cut open. When she asked the nurse what had happened and she was informed that he had a surgery and was on his way to another surgery to amputate his leg because they found a blood clot on his thigh, it had burst before they could get him to the operating

room and the poison got in his blood stream, and that's what caused his death. Everyone left and started preparing for the funeral.

Chapter 14

Darcella finally graduated from high school, and she moved in with the guy that she had been dating for a while, Cassandra didn't approve of it because she felt that he wasn't good enough for her daughter, he was abusive and his family was heavy in the drug game, and she was worried about her daughter and grandchildren. Darcella had two more kids by her man, giving her a total of five children. Cassandra felt sorry for her grandchildren because it was like they were in prison. He wouldn't allow Darcella or her kids to leave the house, but he took good care of she and her children. He ended up going to prison, and Darcella was able to get away from him and once again enjoy her life.

******

After Cassandra's father died, she and her brother's ex-wife Patricia began to hang out together. Patricia and her sister were both into writing bad checks for extra money and told Cassandra about how easy it was. Cassandra was afraid at first, but Patricia continued to tell her how she could write the checks, what she could do with them, and even showed her how to open a checking account. Cassandra was still afraid, so she threw the first set of checks away. She had heard of other people doing it and what they were able to buy and one day she needed food and decided to try it and got away with it. For once Cassandra felt that she could finally help her family by writing the checks and decided that she would go shopping for all her grandkids because they needed a lot of things especially clothes and shoes. Ever since they had moved out, she wasn't able to do as much for them, so she wrote another check, and she did it again, and again, and again with the help of others. This became an addiction.

During all of this, Jasmine had broken up with the father of her son and had met a new guy that she was madly in love with, and they were planning her wedding, Vivian and James had both become very ill. James had a liver disease and was admitted into ICU, and although Vivian was very ill also with a drinking problem, liver problems, high blood pressure and diabetes, she and Cassandra were in the waiting room taking turns checking on him every day for most of the day for two weeks straight. One Tuesday afternoon Vivian and Cassandra went to visit James and noticed that someone had brought him a balloon that was shaped like a cat, and it was moving from one side of the room to the other. There was no air or heat on, but it was moving, it was like it was a spirit or something. James was laying there just looking around not saying much so they walked back to the waiting room to talk amongst each other. Cassandra hated to see her brother like this. She sat down on a chair with both hands covering her face and something told her to go back into the room and when she did James was bleeding from his nose and mouth. When she tried to sit him up, so he wouldn't choke on his blood, she noticed blood in the middle of the bed, she pulled the sheet back a little and realized that he was bleeding from his rectum also. She frantically pushed the call button on his hospital bed to call for the nurse. As they looked into each other's eyes, his eyes filled with tears, and she began to cry. She ran to the waiting room, brushing past the nurse, to get her mother and noticed Gale had arrived she told them what was going on, Vivian and Cassandra ran back to the room while Gale called his wife. By the time everyone arrived he was bleeding very badly - he was dying. He couldn't talk but he looked over at the life support machine as to tell them to pull the plug and just let him go. His wife made the decision, and the doctor pulled the plug, if they would have let him live, he would have been a vegetable and they knew that he would not want to live like that. He looked at them as if to say, *'love you,'* and twenty minutes later he died. Everyone broke down screaming and crying. Cassandra took her mother home where she stayed with her for a couple of day while they prepared for his funeral.

This was so depressing to everyone, and everyone was supposed to be so happy because Jasmine was to get married that Saturday. James was buried on a Thursday afternoon. Vivian was in a daze at the funeral. She just sat there showing no emotions, and when they returned to the church to eat dinner after the burial she just picked at her food. She believed in God and knew that He should not be questioned, but how could he put one person through so much at one time? After Vivian returned home from the funeral, she refused leave the house until they forced her to go to Jasmine's wedding which was beautiful. Her husband was very handsome and looked even better in the white tuxedo with a red shirt underneath and a red handkerchief in his right pocket. Jasmine wore a beautiful white, lacey dress that trailed over the carpet as she walked down the aisle. With all that had happened in the past few days you would have never known because you would not have been able to wipe the smile off of Jasmine's face if you tried. Vivian, who was seated in the second row with some of the immediate family brooding, still showing no emotions, she just sat there starring off into space. It looked like she was dead, she never moved a muscle. Cassandra moved closer to her mother and wrapped her arm around her mother's shoulder.
"What's wrong mom? Don't Jasmine look beautiful? She reminds me so much of you."
Vivian just sat there still not moving.

"I want to go home." Vivian uttered with her mouth in a firm line. Cassandra felt so sorry for her mother, she knew that she was hurting deep inside and there was nothing that she could do. After the wedding and before the reception Vivian's cousin took her home along with her great-grandchildren, and they all stayed with her for the remaining of the evening.

A few months had passed, and Vivian was sulking and began to get sick and sicker as time progressed. She had begun to drink even heavier than she had after John had passed. She was in and out of the hospital for all different kinds of reasons and was finally admitted. When she was released, she wasn't supposed to be alone, so she moved in with Patricia, considering she was always home, and she felt close to her son there. Medicare had a hospital bed and all her medications and supplied shipped there, and she was set up in a room off the living room where she could be checked on periodically and could have access to the kitchen if needed.

It was beginning to snow, and Cassandra unexpectedly went by to visit her mother and found her lying in her bed with a bottle of whisky.
"Mom, what are you doing?"
"What do you want Cassandra?"

"I came by to see how you were doing, but I see that you must be feeling better since you got that bottle up to your mouth."
"Leave me alone." Cassandra grabbed the bottle of whisky from her mother and threw it across the room hitting the wall and shattering. "Mom, you don't need this shit, this is going to be the cause of your death." Cassandra had never cursed at her mother, but she had already lost her father and her brother and didn't want to lose her mother the same way. Cassandra cleaned up the mess and went back home to relax her mind.

    Christmas was approaching and Patricia and her kids were decorating the house, putting up the tree, cutting celery, bell peppers, onions and gizzards for the dressing, baking cakes and cookies. This holiday spirit made Vivian felt so much better, and on Christmas day she got up, put on a nice pair of slacks and a sparkling sweater, ate dinner and sat in the living room and watched television with her grandchildren for the first time since she had been in that house. That evening when Vivian went to bed, she started feeling sick again and the day before New Year's she was worst then she had ever been, her breathing wasn't good, and she had rattling in her chest every time she took a breath. She didn't go to the hospital this time and on January 2nd Vivian was pronounced dead at 4:00 pm, she had drunk herself to death. Her funeral was packed, no one could believe that she was gone, she was such a sweet and loving person that would do anything for anyone and always had her door open for someone who needed a place to stay, and now she was gone.

Chapter 15

Cassandra became very depressed and began to see a doctor and was given medication to keep her mind right, but the pills made her think evil especially when it came to men. She just wasn't in her right mind, always wanted to fight, and didn't want to be bothered with anyone. She started writing more checks, she didn't know what was happening, she wasn't her kind loving self anymore. Every time she closed her eyes, she had visions of her father laying on top of her saying *"let me see if you've been messing with someone"* when all the time it was him. She began thinking back about her past relationships and the men that had hurt her and she wanted to hurt every one of them. She wanted to crawl into a cage, alone so she could never be hurt again.

Sometime in the summer of 1995 Cassandra was arrested for some of the checks that she had written and was in jail for three days because it was a city holiday. All the women welcomed her with open arms, they were nice to her and made her feel comfortable, but this was not where she wanted to be. She had become extremely ill being in there and she continued to hear her dad's voice in her head *"I got you now and there is nowhere for you to run."* She was

terrified, she couldn't breathe and wanted to crawl in a corner and be left alone. The following Tuesday she went to court and told the truth about writing the checks. She wanted this to all be over with. She was released to Mr. Aaron Mead, her probation officer, and placed on probation for ten years under controlled supervision. Her probation officer was a tall light-brown skinned man with a nice brush cut and a well-trimmed mustache. The first time she went to see him, she didn't trust him, it was something about him that just didn't feel right but she couldn't put her finger on it. He would stare at her in a way that made her feel uncomfortable, and she knew it was wrong.
"Wow, Ms. Woods, you sure are a pretty woman."
"Thanks." She replied with a half of a smile feeling uncomfortable. He explained to her what the rules were and what he expected out of her, and she continued to see him once a week. After about a month he started hinting around that he wanted to have an affair with her, and when she acted as if she didn't know what he was talking about, he started being mean to her and trying to use his authority to control her.
"Ms. Woods, you know I could send you to prison, right?"
"For what?" She asked.
"Because I am a probation officer." He said pointing to his identification tag on his shirt. "And you have to follow my rules." She just sat

there with a distraught look on her face thinking. *"I thought that being a pretty girl was a good thing, I hate this. Maybe if I were ugly these things wouldn't happen to me."* She didn't understand why everything that involved her had to have a bad ending. Wasn't she a child of God, too? Why did this stuff continue to happen? Every time she went to see him, he told her how pretty she was, and now she hated those words together.

"You know Cassandra I've been thinking about you since the day that we met, and I want you to be my lady."

"What do you mean by that?" *Oh no, what was she going to do? She needed to get out of there, fast, and find a way so that she never had to come back.*

"Don't play no kid games with me, you know what I want."

"Look, I'm just trying to do my time I have to do and get on with my life."

"You have a long time to come and see me, we might as well make it worth something." He pulled out his chart. "Man, ten years, if we lived together, we would have a common law marriage." He began to laugh as he reached over and rubbed her leg.

"I don't know what you want, but I did my visit for this week and now I'm leaving." Cassandra got up and got her things and tried to leave, but he pushed her up against the wall and began to kiss her in the mouth. She pushed him away and ran out of the office. The next few weeks she went to see him, she wore a pair of baggy jeans, a big sweatshirt, her hair in curlers and a head scarf trying to turn him off, but it didn't work.

"So, is that how you look when you get up in the morning? That's crazy you are beautiful even at your worst." Cassandra didn't reply. They finished their official business, and she was about to leave.

"Next week when you come, I need you to bring me a photo of you."

"For what?"

"Because I need it, and it needs to be nude."

"Boy, you done lost your mind."

"You are going to lose yours if I don't get those photos because I'm going to send you to Marysville for the remainder of your probation. You think it was hard in the county jail, just wait until you are in prison. It's no walk in the park, and nine and a half years, man, sucks to be you." Cassandra looked at him and his smirk on his face; he was a real asshole. The cage came to her mind as she starred at him, all she could think about was that she was going to be raped and beat up again like her childhood and past relationship. What else could she do? She felt her only option was to bring him the picture. She was trying to put all of this behind her so that she could be a better person, but she couldn't with all of these obstacles, she wanted to change and better herself for her children and grandchildren. She needed them, and they needed her, they were all that she loved. She wanted to be a positive role model for them, but she just couldn't seem to move forward. At this point she wanted to die, she went home and took a hand full of pills and lay down, and she felt as if she was flying as she dozed off. Several hours later she woke up with a pounding headache - she didn't die - she hadn't taken enough pills, or the good Lord just wasn't ready for her. Now the thought of taking those pictures for that sick bastard or going to prison for nine years haunted her, even if she went to court and told how he was threatening her, would they believe her? She had a history of theft, and that fits in the same category as being a liar, and it would be her word against his. The next day she called a friend over, not explaining anything, and had her take the pictures.

    The following week she went to meet with Mr. Mead with the pictures tucked away in her purse. They did their business, going over files and paperwork and she was about to leave. She got up from the chair and was headed for the door."
"Leaving so soon, Ms. Cassandra? I think you're forgetting something." Her back was to him so he couldn't see her face; she softly closed her eyes and inhaled as she turned around with a fake smile on her face.
"Oh, what did I forget?" He smiled back.

"Don't play with me. Where are my pictures?" he asked as the smile slowly faded from his face.
"Are you really going to do this?"
"I told you what I wanted, and I meant it." Cassandra shook her head as she went through her purse to retrieve the pictures. She got them and threw them on the floor.
"Oh, that's how you're acting?" She didn't reply. "You need to pick those up."
"I'm not, if you want them, you pick them up yourself because if I get them, they are going home with me." Mr. Mead bent down and picked up the pictures, and she turned to walk away. "Hold up don't leave yet, let me see what I have here." He opened the envelope, and a big smile grew across his face. "Oh, these are beautiful." He grabbed her by the arm and pulled her close, but she didn't move, so he moved in closer to her and grabbed her into his arms and kissed her on the neck, and she never budged. "This is beautiful. I knew you cared about my needs." Cassandra didn't reply, she pulled away and left his presence. Cassandra cried most of the way home feeling dirty and humiliated. She went to visit her daughter and took her oldest granddaughter home to spend a couple of days with her so she wouldn't be alone and to keep her mind occupied.

A few days had gone by, and Cassandra had put the picture situation in the back of her

mind. She was enjoying her granddaughter. There was a knock at the door, she walked to the door singing 'Jesus loves me,' and when she reached the living room, she could see it was a man, but he had his back turned. She stopped singing and as she got closer, she noticed that it was Mr. Mead.
"I don't have a meeting with you today. What are you doing here?"
"I just came to see if you really live here and make sure you weren't doing anything you don't have any business."
"I don't think that what I do on my spare time is any of your business as long as when it's time for me to drop urine it's clean, and as long as I don't get in any trouble you don't need to worry about what I do."
"Don't be so hostile, it just part of my job. Are you going to open the door?"
"No."
"Cassandra, why do you always make things so difficult? I'm just trying to do my job here." Cassandra unlocked the screen door, and Mr. Mead came in. "Oh, you have a beautiful home. Do you mind if I look around?"
"Yes, I do mind. I'm busy right now, and I don't recall reading anything about you just popping up at my house."
"It's something new we are trying," he said as he walked close to her. He reached for her arm just as her granddaughter Cheryl came running around the corner.

"Granny, look at the picture I made for you." Mr. Mead let his hands fall to his side and a disappointed look came across his face as the little girl entered the room.

"Well, Ms. Woods, I'm not going to keep you, it looks like everything is alright here. I'll see you at the meeting next week." He said as he winked at her.

"Oh, Granny, who was that?"

"Just some man baby, nothing to worry about. Now let me see that picture you made for me, and it better not be a picture of me looking old and fat again." They both began to laugh as she hugged her granddaughter.

Chapter 16

One afternoon Cassandra was taking the curlers out of her hair getting ready for a date with Nathaniel, when she heard a knock on the door. She figured it must have been either one of her children or her granddaughter, so she hurried to the door. When she looked out of the beige and white curtains with roosters lining the bottom, she saw two unfamiliar faces. "Yes, may I help you? Cassandra yelled through the closed door.
"Cassandra Woods?" called one of the women. Cassandra stood there wondering who they were and what they could possibly want. "Can you open the door? We need to talk with you about an important matter."
"Cassandra isn't here. I can tell her you came by."
"Miss Woods, we know it's you. We are not here to arrest you; we just want to ask you a few questions about Mr. Mead." Cassandra stood there a few more seconds, and the other woman showed her badge, "We are detectives Miss Woods, please open the door."
Cassandra took a deep breath and opened the door and in walked in one short chubby dark-complexed woman with a Hallie Berry haircut and a tall caramel-complexed woman with straight shoulder length hair. They walked into

the living room and complemented her on her home.

"May we have a seat?" Cassandra motioned her hands toward the olive-green sofa. "I'm Detective Melody, and this is my partner Detective Jody." The tall caramel-complexed woman said. Cassandra continued to pace the floor. "Could you please take a seat?" Detective Jody asked. Cassandra did as she was asked.

"The reason that we stopped by today was to inform you that Mr. Mead has been passing nude pictures of you around the police station, and we had saw them. Cassandra put her head down in shame.

"We have already contacted the head of the Probation Department and we need to know how all of this transpired." Cassandra just sat there not knowing what to say.

"It's okay Cassandra; this is for your best interest." Tears streamed down Cassandra's face. Detective Melody stood up and went over to the chair that Cassandra was sitting in and put her arm around her shoulder.

"I understand that you may be embarrassed, but what do he say or do to you to make you send those pictures?" Cassandra took a deep breath and started from the beginning. She told them how he started by touching her leg during their meetings, then telling her how pretty she was, which lead to him asking her out, and when she refused, he threatened to send her to prison. She told how he had kissed her and

came to her home when her granddaughter was there, and finally how he ended up demanding the pictures. They continued to question her and then asked her to come downtown to try to set him up by calling him in hopes that he would answer the phone. She knew he probably wouldn't talk to her because the previous Friday he had called her and told her not to call him at his office anymore because he was under investigation, and they would probably find her a new probation officer. He wouldn't explain what was going on; he just told her that she needed to follow those rules. Cassandra grabbed her jacket and got into the back seat of the detective's car and rode downtown. When they arrived, they took her back into this room with all these computers, phones and tape recorders, and she felt extremely nervous and uncomfortable. They called him several times, but he refused to take her call, so she was instructed to leave him a message and was told that if he called her back, she was to set up a meeting with him somewhere and to contact them to let them know the time and location. Two days later Mr. Mead called Cassandra at about 6:30 in the morning, she was up doing laundry and was wondering who was calling her this early.
"Hello."
"Cassandra, look I got your message, they are watching me, so please don't call me anymore."

"What's goin…" He hung up. She was about to call him back but decided against it.

   Two to three weeks had passed, and Cassandra had a new probation officer, and her name was Mrs. Butler, a short, older, Caucasian woman who was strictly business. She hadn't heard anything from Mr. Mead or the Detectives and tried to ask Mrs. Butler about Mr. Mead, but she just redirected to question back to their business. When she arrived home that afternoon there was a letter in her mailbox with a court date - the state had pressed charges against Mr. Mead. She didn't feel like going through this mess, but what else could she do? Mr. Mead was placed on administrative leave, then arrested, and was now out on bail. On their court date, Cassandra wore a nice three-piece suit because her parents always told her to look her best when she went before the judge. Mr. Mead entered the court room after Cassandra was already seated, he came in with his attorney and the reverend from the local church, they began the hearing, and Mr. Mead had told the reverend that he was set up so he spoke on his behalf telling the court how nice of a guy that Mr. Mead was, how he would never do anything like that, and how this must be a misunderstanding. Mr. Mead was fired, they couldn't set him up because they didn't have enough evidence to prosecute him, but the pictures were enough for him to lose his job.

Cassandra had tried to get an attorney of her own, but considering she was already on probation, her creditability wasn't any good, so no one wanted to take her case. There was one attorney in Cleveland, but he wanted two thousand dollars up front. She didn't have the money, so she just let the case go. Mr. Mead moved to Cleveland, Ohio, and was not longer permitted to work as a Probation Officer, anywhere.

Chapter 17

Cassandra and Nathaniel were seeing each other more often now, but they were having problems, and it was her fault because she said she was committed but was still doing her own thing. One night she had invited him over, and he rejected her. She became suspicious and assumed that he was having another woman come to his apartment. Cassandra decided to go out with her friends to try to get her mind off Nathaniel for the night, but she couldn't. She put on a red three-piece suit, black panty hose and a pair of red and gold pumps, and she knew that she looked sexy. She arrived at the club and several men were checking her out, but she continued to have butterflies in her stomach thinking about what Nathaniel may have been doing. She tried to drink her thoughts away, but it only made matters worse. There were so many attractive men out that night drinking and having a good time, but in her mind none of them could compare to Nathaniel, and she found no interest in any of them and continued drinking.

After several hours of drinking and partying, Cassandra couldn't enjoy herself, so she decided it was time to go. When she got up to go home, she realized that she had too much to drink. She dropped her friends off and decided to go pay her man a visit. When she arrived, she entered the building, got on the elevator and pushed the number three. When she arrived at the third floor, she fumbled with her keys trying to find her key to enter his apartment, and they dropped to the floor. When she found the key and tried it the door was unlocked, but it was like someone was holding the handle so she couldn't turn the knob. She pushed on the door and continued to try to open it, but it was no use. She knew someone was there because she could hear the television and people talking and shuffling around on the other side of the door, so she headed back downstairs and headed to her car. When she reached her car, she turned around and looked up at his apartment and saw lights flashing, and she knew it his television so now she knew he was in there and that he was in the living room, and he wasn't alone. She knew his routine.

Cassandra locked her car and headed towards the balcony. She took off her shoes, threw them over the balcony, and began to climb up the first railing. It was extremely hard, but she was determined. She proceeded to climb the second railing, which was much easier because she was able to use the first railing to make her higher off the ground. When she was at the top of the second balcony she threw her purse, shoes and jacket onto his balcony and proceeded to climb up. When she finally was at her destination she was exhausted, but when

she looked through the window and saw Nathanial and some woman lying in the living room on a blow-up mattress, she forgot about being tired. She knocked on the window.
"Open the door!" She yelled. She saw the lady get up, grab her clothes, and run into the bathroom. Cassandra began kicking the window trying to bust it out. A man that lived in the building was standing on the ground looking up at Cassandra.
"Are you alright, ma'am?" he asked.
"I'm fine," she said without looking back and he walked away. She kicked the door real hard with her bare foot, and it finally shattered, then she took the side of her body and rammed it up against the glass. It broke, and she fell through it cutting her leg and arm. She ignored her wounds and ran toward the bathroom, but the lady would not come out.
"Cassandra, what are you doing here?"
"What do you mean?"
"What do you want?" We are not together; we are just friends."
"Yes, we are."
"We are not."
"Since when?"
"Cassandra, you shouldn't have come by here."
"I thought that was the purpose of me having a key."
"You need to leave."
"No, tell your little whore to come out of the bathroom."

"She's not coming out until you leave."
"Well, I guess she'll be in here all night because I'm not going nowhere. What is she doing here anyways?"
"Cassandra, would you just leave? I'll call you later."
"I know you're not choosing her over me." Cassandra got up and ran to the bathroom and began to bang on the door and tried to open the door.
"Stop being a coward and come on out. You were laid up all comfortable when I looked in the window, so don't be shy now." She turned to Nathanial. "Look, I have to pee, you need to make her come out of there right now." She folded her arms and leaned up against the wall next to the bathroom door.
"Cassandra, stop acting like that, you can't go in there right now so just wait, as a matter of fact, you need to leave right now." Cassandra walked towards the living room and sat on the arm of the couch.
"I can't hold it any longer, and if you don't let me go in there then I'm going to pee right here on your couch." Nathanial came close to Cassandra, and she moved over to sit on the cushion of the couch, and before she could sit down, she urinated through her clothes and onto his sofa. "I told you I couldn't hold it anymore."
"I don't believe you really just did that." Nathanial walked into his bedroom and lied back on the bed trying to get his thoughts

together and figure out how he could get his female friend out of his apartment because he knew it was no use in trying to get Cassandra to leave or to even act civil. He slowly walked to the hallway and took Cassandra's hand and walked her into his bedroom.
"Come on, let's talk." Cassandra followed him into his bedroom, and he laid her down on the bed and then he hurdled over her so she couldn't get up. "Baby RUN." The bathroom door slowly opened, and the lady peeked her head around the corner and when she saw them on the bed she ran out of the apartment. Cassandra took a shower and stayed the night with the man that, in the back of her mind, was one day going to be all hers.

Surprisingly the next morning, as soon as Cassandra got dressed and went home, Nathanial went downtown to the police department and filed a restraining order against her. They were still cordial, but he refused to let her continue to come to his apartment and try to run things. If they were going to continue to mess around, it was going to be on his terms.

Chapter 18

Nathanial was still a ladies' man and had female friends that he spent time with, and Cassandra didn't like their arrangements. She wanted him to herself, and not only when it was convenient for him. She would pop up at his apartment periodically, but he continued to remind her of the restraining order that he had against her. She was not trying to go back to jail for anyone. She loved him more than he could ever imagine but wasn't willing to sacrifice her freedom for his affection.

Cassandra decided it was only fair if he could have friends that she should be able to also. She finally decided to go out with a couple of guys that had been trying to hook up with her in the past. They took her out to dinner or to the club a few times, but it was never anything serious. She wanted Nathanial and was just using these other guys to occupy her mind, for their money, and to keep her self-esteem up, reminding herself that she was still beautiful and could get another man.

Eric Jr. had returned home from college and was staying with his mother until he found a job and place of his own, and Cassandra was so happy to have her son back that she did any and everything for him to make him comfortable. She washed his clothes, cooked for him, washed his dishes, and kept the room that he was sleeping in clean. Eventually he found a place of his own, and she was devastated that her son was leaving her again, so she moved right across the parking lot from him. She wanted to keep her son close to her and make sure that he didn't want or need anything. Eric Jr. kept her mind occupied and off Nathanial. She would cook dinner for him and take it to him a few times a week and even go into his apartment when he was at work to tidy up things - anything to keep busy. A couple of times a week she held hand dancing classes in her basement to make extra money and again to occupy her time.

    Several months had passed and Cassandra was about to turn the big 5-0 and was planning a big party. She and Nathanial were still friends with benefits, and he would spend the night with her here and there, so she invited him to her party, and he came. She put on a pair of skintight jeans, a pink blouse, and her hair and make-up were flawless. She was so happy and blessed to have reached the age of fifty and didn't look a day over forty, so to have Nathanial there just made her day much brighter. After the party ended and everyone left, Cassandra talked Nathanial into spending the night with her and he didn't hesitate. After that night they decided to finally be a couple, but not until after he returned from a trip that he had planned with one of his female friends. Cassandra wasn't happy about that at all, but what could she do? They already had their airline tickets and hotel reservations. She was hurt and disappointed but set back and waited for her man to return. It was hard because she continued to think about what they could have been doing all night. Although he had told her that they had never messed around because he was thinking about her every time they got together. She believed him because she had no choice, and she loved him so much that she would have believed him if her told her the sky was pink. She finally took a sleeping pill and dozed off to sleep. Monday afternoon, as promised, when his plane landed, he was back with Cassandra. She didn't believe that he would be there for long, because they had been through this same scenario more times than she could count during the past twenty-five years, but she was going to enjoy the moment while it lasted.

    Surprising after Cassandra and Nathanial talked and started spending more time together, they became close like they were when they first met, and they got along so well. There was so much more love and romance that she didn't know what to do with herself. She hadn't really thought about her father that much until Eric, the father of her children died. Although they had barely spoken to each other, it still hurt inside to see the man that she once loved and the father of her children laying in a coffin. The funeral was so sad to watch her children and her grandchildren cry for the loss of this man, but she had Nathanial to keep her together. He didn't attend the funeral but gave Cassandra his shoulder to cry on upon her return.

    Eric Jr. moved out of his apartment and into his father's house on the other side of town, and Cassandra was finally tired of all the close neighbors hearing everything they did, when they took a shower, arguing and everything else, and she wasn't too fond of staying in that neighborhood without her son close, so she moved into a house in a better part of town. She continued to hold her dance classes, and she and Nathanial were getting along great, he even attended a few of her classes. One year later they decided to move in together. Cassandra couldn't believe this was finally happening, she finally had someone whom she felt really loved her and cared about her well-being, and she was not going to let this end. They began to go to church every Sunday, and several months later they began to discuss getting married. March 2004, they began planning their wedding, and that August Cassandra was the happiest bride in the world.

    The day of the wedding, Cassandra was so nervous that she had to go have a few drinks before the wedding to ease her mind, and

when she returned Nathaniel had a white Navigator limousine pick her up from their home and take her to the church. The driver left while she got ready and later returned with the groom and the best man. She wore an off-white gown with pearl sequins, a long veil which also contained pearls, pearl gloves, pearl earrings and necklace. She made a beautiful bride but was still nervous. Eric Jr., who gave her away, was sitting with his mother talking while they were waiting for her cue to walk down the aisle, and he noticed that his mother looked troubled.
"What's wrong with you?" He asked as he put his hand on her shoulder.
"Nothing." She lied; she was thinking about the man that she was going to marry. Was he going to treat her like the other men in her life? She wanted to cry at the thought, but before a tear could fall, they came and got her, it was her time to walk down the aisle. Eric Jr. continued to ask her if she was alright, she wasn't, but didn't say it, and as she walked down the aisle it was like someone had lifted her off her feet and she was floating to her soon to be husband. When she saw him standing there, she wanted to pinch herself to make sure this wasn't a dream, he was so handsome standing there in his white tuxedo, with a white cane, hat and shoes waiting for his wife. Her sister, Gale was the matron of honor. Darcella was the bridesmaid, and Jasmine didn't want to be in the wedding, so she just

helped with all the miscellaneous things. Her great-granddaughter, Darcella's three-year-old granddaughter, was the flower girl, she wore a white dress and had a veil too. Her grandson and his friend rolled down the carpet and escorted the people to their seats. Cassandra had them play 'Beneath my wings' by Levert, dedicating it to her deceased father, and 'Sweet Sadie' by the Spinners for her mother. Everything was so beautiful, and her family was so supportive. They both wrote their own vows, and Cassandra poured her heart out to him telling him when they first met, she knew it was meant to be and that one day they would be where they were at the time, standing at the altar. Nathaniel expressed how much he cherished and appreciated her and how their love would be never ending. After the wedding they returned to the Navigator that also had a sunroof big enough for them both to stand up in. They rolled through the city waving at people as the driver blew the horn. They went to a lake, which was perfect for this beautiful sunny day, and took their pictures and then stopped by the liquor store to get drinks for those who drank, which excluded Nathaniel. They finally arrived at the beautiful hall where the reception was held, and the place was set up so nice. There were white and silver balloons everywhere, each table had a glass vase with white marbles, with white and red flowers. The food was delicious. They had salad, baked chicken, green beans, fried corn, sweet potatoes and dinner rolls, the caterer did a lovely job. They danced and had a great time, the night turned out to be one of the best days of her life. She had the man that she was trying to get for almost thirty years, and he was now her husband. They say good things come to those who wait. Or do they?

Afterward

After the wedding was final, they continued to go to church and even joined the Ministry together. She started teaching Sunday school to the children and he joined several committees in the church and even though things were going well, she just couldn't forget her past, and that sometimes-caused problems with loving him the way that she wanted to. She did a lot of things that weren't right, like getting money from her husband telling him it was for one thing but then using it to help her children, grandchildren or for whatever else she wanted. She wanted her life to be different and she trusted him, but she was always looking over her shoulder because of the things that all the men that had been in her life had done to her in the past. With God's help, she was hoping to put all of this behind her and be able to reach out to someone who has been through the same things that she has experienced. What Cassandra went through is a serious matter, and it will take over your life without professional help.

Without God, the presence of her children and grandchildren, and the support of her loving friend, whom she married, Cassandra would have never made it.

Also check out other books by

D M Cummings:

Diamond's Pearl ISBN 9780977385416 ($13.95), Is a blunt but urban epic starring Diamond, a girl whose life is turned inside out because of her mother's austere rules and the fact that she felt like the black sheep of the family. Her older sister and younger brother were very aloof when it came to Diamond, and she hadn't seen her father since she was a youth. This led to her becoming promiscuous, looking for love in all the wrong places, which landed her with a child to whom the father was unknown.

Is Real Love Worth My Life? ISBN 9780977385409 ($13.95), Is a story of love and hate. It tells how a girl will stay around when her man puts it down no matter what he put her through. It talks about the life of being 'the man's' girl, domestic violence and the twisted things that people will do when they think they are in love.

Introduction

It's been almost 10 years since Mike and I met and I'll be damned if I let his six old baby mamas', his two new baby mama's or a few ass whippings here or there tear us apart. He owes me; I've given up everything for him, the love of my life, my dream of having a family, not just a baby daddy, and basically my life. I've given him everything that he's asked for even a pretty, little girl, even though it jeopardized my relationship with my friends and family.

I learned how to live with his other women and the smacks in the mouth when I asked him about them. The lies all became reality. The kids coming out of the woodwork became my kids. My friends distanced themselves from me because every time we went out, he would bust out my car windows or we would be fighting, but I still stayed with him even when he slashed two of my tires and left me in the roughest projects in Akron in the middle of the night when I was four months pregnant. But through all of this, he was there for me in my time of need, he showed me love and gave me sexual healing. Although we weren't married, Mike was in it for the long run, until death do us part. He's going to repay me with his life for all the blood, all the tears, every headache, heartbreak, all the love that I have given him and the ten years that I did nothing but catered to his ass. Or is it worth it?

These books are available on Amazon, BN.com and you can visit at www.reallovedmc.com for online specials. You can also send check or money order in the amount of $13.95 plus $3.95 for shipping and handling to:

The World Is Mine (TWIM) Publishing
PO Box 3086
Akron, Oh 44309